Introduction

Five Steps to Test Success

You have been preparing for the GED Social Studies Test by reviewing social studies topics that you already know and learning even more about them.

As you get closer to taking the GED, it makes sense to ask, "What steps should I take to make sure that I pass the GED Social Studies Test?" That's where this book comes in. This book doesn't teach you about social studies—instead, it teaches you about the GED Social Studies Test. *Pass the GED™ Social Studies Test* is a valuable companion to other GED study materials. But unlike those other books, videos, or software, its only job is to help you figure out how to achieve your goal—passing the test.

This book takes you through the **Five Steps to GED Test Success:**

Step 1: Know What To Expect on the Test
Get clear on such basic issues as how many questions are on the test and how long you have to answer them. Find out what kind of social studies background you need and what types of test questions you can expect.

Step 2: Practice Social Studies Thinking Skills
Questions on the GED Social Studies Test are different from those you may remember from school such as, "When did the United States enter World War I?" The GED does not test your recall of social studies facts. Instead, it evaluates how well you can use thinking skills to interpret social studies information. The Step 2 section of this book explains the thinking skills and shows you how to answer questions that require you to use each of the different thinking skills.

Step 3: Practice Social Studies Graphic Skills
About half of the questions on the GED Social Studies Test are based on tables, timelines, graphs, maps, cartoons, and photos similar to those in social studies textbooks and articles. As you sharpen your ability to interpret social studies graphics, you will take another step toward passing the test.

Step 4: Practice Taking the GED
There's nothing like the real thing. This section will help you ease into test-taking mode with a *Practice Test Warm-Up.* Then, you will take a full-length *Practice GED Social Studies Test.* You will answer questions similar to those on the real test. You'll take the Practice Test in the same amount of time you'll be given for the real test.

Step 5: Make Your Plan for Test Success
At the end of this book, you will have a chance to make a plan based on all that you've learned about the GED Test and about yourself. You and your teacher may decide that you are ready to take the GED Social Studies Test. Or, you may need more time to develop your skills. Use the *GED Personal Coach™* on pages 38–39 to make your final plan.

Besides providing you with lots of test advice and practice, this book will occasionally ask you to STOP AND THINK. We will ask you to explain why you chose an answer to a question. We will ask you to think about how you are doing and how you can improve. Make the most of these opportunities, and you will see your test performance increase dramatically! Now, on to Step 1 ...

Step 1: Know What To Expect on the Test

Frequently Asked Questions About the GED Social Studies Test

Q: How many questions are on the GED Social Studies Test? How long do I have to answer them?
A: There are 50 questions on the test. You will have 70 minutes, which is 1 hour and 10 minutes, to answer them. When you consider that two or three questions are often based on the same graphic or passage, you can see that you will have plenty of time to finish the test.

Q: What types of questions are on the test?
A: There are only multiple-choice questions on the GED Social Studies Test. Each question has five answer choices, and you must pick the correct one.

Q: If I don't know the answer to a question, should I guess or should I skip it?
A: Don't skip any questions. If you are not sure of the answer, eliminate the choices that are clearly wrong and make a guess by choosing from the remaining choices.

Q: What social studies facts do I need to memorize to pass the test?
A: You don't need to memorize any specific social studies facts to pass the GED Social Studies Test.

Q: If I don't have to memorize any facts, do I need to know any social studies to pass?
A: It's helpful to know highlights of U.S. and world history. It's also helpful to be familiar with the structure of American government and to have basic knowledge of economics and world geography.

Knowledge of social studies is helpful because it's much easier to correctly interpret social studies passages and graphics if you have some basic knowledge to build on. Still, you can sometimes figure out the correct answer to a question by reading the passage or graphic carefully, even if you've never encountered the specific topic before.

Q: I hear that the GED tests social studies thinking skills. What does that mean?
A: That means that you'll be expected to think critically when answering questions. You'll have to understand what you read and recognize facts. But you will also need to interpret information and recognize points of view, opinions, values, and assumptions. Many topics in social studies are open to interpretation.

Q: I hear that there are lots of graphics on the test. What can I expect to see?
A: You will see tables and charts, which organize information in a grid. A chart might compare the powers of the president in the United States and France. A special type of chart, called a timeline, shows historic events in chronological order. You may also see diagrams and drawings.

You can expect to see line graphs, bar graphs, and circle graphs. Graphs show numeric data, such as the consumer price index for a five-year period or the number of votes each candidate won in a presidential election.

You will also see maps. Maps can show the location of physical features, political boundaries, and many other types of information. Finally, you will see cartoons and photos. Cartoons use humor to present opinions about various aspects of current events. Photos capture the essence of a historic event or period with memorable images.

Q: What historic documents should I be familiar with? What practical documents might I see on the test?

A: The historic documents that are quoted most often on the test are the U.S. Declaration of Independence and the Constitution. In addition, there may be excerpts from famous political speeches or important U.S. Supreme Court decisions. See page 45 for an overview of some important historic documents. The test also includes quotes from and questions about a practical document. Practical documents could include a voter's guide, a tax form, a consumer information document, and so on.

Q: What is a passing score on the GED Social Studies Test?

A: You need two different scores to pass the GED. You will need a PASSING score of at least* 410 for the Social Studies Test and an AVERAGE of at least* 450 for all five tests. To get a score of 450 on the Social Studies Test, you need to get about 35 questions correct.

However, it is important that you set a higher goal for yourself. Because you need 450 as an average on all of the tests, you should try to get as many correct answers as possible so that you can beat the average score on each test. To earn your GED certificate, you will need "above average" scores on some tests to compensate for possible "below average" scores on other tests.

Q: How will this book help me pass the GED Social Studies Test?

A: This book will familiarize you with the GED Social Studies Test—what's on it, how to interpret passages and graphics, and how to answer questions. It will also help you figure out the best approach to taking the test for you personally. The more you know about the test, and the more you know about test-taking strategies, the more prepared you will be to do well.

Q: What else can I do to pass the GED Social Studies Test?

A: Listen to the news on radio and TV and read articles in newspapers and magazines. Today's news is tomorrow's history, so you can learn a lot about U.S. and world history and geography just by keeping up with current events. Often the media will provide background stories on the history of a region when that region is in the news. In addition, stories about economics, politics, and government are in the news every day. Follow the news, and you'll learn a lot.

* These numbers are the minimum scores set by the GED Testing Service. Individual states and provinces may set <u>higher</u> PASSING and/or AVERAGE scores. Talk to your teacher or contact your state's Department of Adult Education to get the passing requirements for your state.

Your Turn

What other questions do you have about the GED Social Studies Test? Write them here or on a separate sheet of paper, and discuss them with your teacher.

_____
_____
_____
_____
_____

Step 2: Practice Social Studies Thinking Skills

Comprehend What You Read

On the GED Social Studies Test, you will have to **comprehend** (understand) social studies ideas in short passages and graphics. You will need to read carefully and select the answer choice that best summarizes, restates, or explains the implication of important social studies information.

EXAMPLE

The nation's first president, George Washington, picked his department secretaries with no regard for their political background. He selected competent men "of known attachment to the government."

Which of the following is suggested by Washington's criteria for selecting advisors?

(1) Washington used his political power mainly to grant favors to his friends.
(2) Washington needed to surround himself with followers who were devoted to him.
(3) Loyalty to one political party was needed in the new government.
(4) The new government was powerful.
(5) For the new government to survive, it needed qualified, loyal leaders.

Answer and Explanations

(1) Nothing in the passage suggests that this is true. Washington selected advisors based on their qualifications, not on friendship.
(2) The passage indicates that Washington picked men who were loyal to the new government, not that he picked men who had shown personal loyalty to him.
(3) The passage states that Washington did not use political background as a criterion for selecting department heads.
(4) Washington's actions suggest the opposite—the new government was not powerful and needed strong leaders to secure its establishment.
(5) **This is correct. The passage states that Washington focused on loyalty to the new nation when selecting department heads. This and Washington's emphasis on competence indicate that his main goal was the government's survival.**

Try It Yourself

A continental divide is an imaginary boundary along a line of mountain peaks. On one side, water flows in one direction; on the other, water flows in the opposite direction. In North America, the continental divide runs through the Rocky Mountains.

Which is the BEST title for the passage?

(1) The Rocky Mountains
(2) An Imaginary Boundary
(3) What Is a Continental Divide?
(4) The Flow of Water
(5) Geographic Boundaries

Think It Through

Which is the correct answer? _____

Why is it correct? Give a specific reason.

_____
_____
_____

Answer and Explanation: The correct answer is **(3) What Is a Continental Divide?** That's because the answer covers the topic of the passage, the continental divide. Choices (1), (2), and (4) are wrong because they focus on details. Choice (5) is incorrect because it is too broad.

Practice

Choose the <u>one best answer</u> to the questions below. Write a short explanation for your answers to questions 1 and 2.

<u>Questions 1 and 2</u> are based on this passage.

The unemployment rate is measured by the Bureau of Labor Statistics (BLS). It counts people as unemployed if they are actively looking for work. However, after a period of job-hunting, some discouraged people stop job-hunting. Unemployed people who aren't looking for work aren't counted in the unemployment rate. They are considered to be outside the labor force altogether.

1. What is the main idea of this passage?

   (1) The BLS collects employment data.
   (2) The BLS classifies the labor force.
   (3) Looking for work can be discouraging.
   (4) The unemployment rate includes only unemployed people looking for work.
   (5) Discouraged job seekers are classified as outside the labor force.

   Answer choice _____

   Explanation _____
   _____

2. What is implied by the passage?

   (1) The BLS gathers data on pay rates.
   (2) The unemployment rate is understated.
   (3) Most job hunters are discouraged.
   (4) Discouraged workers eventually reenter the labor force.
   (5) Most people find a job within a month.

   Answer choice _____

   Explanation _____
   _____

<u>Questions 3 and 4</u> are based on this passage.

A presidential candidate may have a campaign organization with several hundred paid workers and thousands of volunteers. The head of the campaign organization is the campaign manager, who coordinates and directs the campaign. A campaign also has many paid consultants. These include the following: political consultants who advise on strategies; media consultants, who make TV, radio, and print ads and manage relations with the press; and pollsters, who take public opinion surveys on behalf of the candidate.

3. What is the BEST title for this passage?

   (1) The Rise of Political Consultants
   (2) The Presidential Campaign Organization
   (3) Volunteers in Campaign Organizations
   (4) How to Be Elected President
   (5) The Campaign Manager

4. What can you infer from the information in this passage?

   (1) To run a presidential campaign, a candidate must have a lot of money.
   (2) Presidential campaigns often last well over a year.
   (3) Most campaign workers work at campaign headquarters.
   (4) A media consultant's job is more difficult than that of a pollster.
   (5) Polling provides unreliable data for the candidate.

Check answers and explanations on page 40.

Apply What You Learn

On the GED Social Studies Test, some questions ask you to **apply,** or use, information. You may be given a general principle and asked to identify a specific example of it. Or you may have to figure out a generalization and then apply it to a specific situation.

EXAMPLE

In a monopoly, one company is the only producer of a product or a service that has no close substitutes. Which of the following is an example of a company with a monopoly?

(1) American Telephone & Telegraph, the nation's only phone company until 1984
(2) General Motors, the nation's largest car manufacturer
(3) Providence Water Supply Board, a city agency that provides water for all local residents and businesses
(4) the Internet, an informal, worldwide communications network of computers
(5) Nokia, a Finnish company that is the world's leading cell phone manufacturer

Answer and Explanations

(1) **This is correct. Before the company was broken up in 1984, the original AT&T was the only U.S. phone service. Since there was no close substitute for phone service, AT&T had a monopoly.**
(2) Many other car manufacturers compete with General Motors. Therefore, GM does not have a monopoly.
(3) Although the Providence Water Supply Board is the only provider of water in Providence, Rhode Island, it is a government agency, not a company. Thus, it is not considered a monopoly.
(4) The Internet is not a monopoly because it is an informal collection of networked computers, not a company.
(5) Many other cell phone manufacturers compete with Nokia. Therefore, Nokia doesn't have a monopoly.

Try It Yourself

Local governments, such as counties and school districts, get their powers from state governments. State governments set their boundaries and determine their powers. Which is MOST similar to the relationship between state and local governments?

The relationship between

(1) mayors and city councils
(2) the federal and state governments
(3) the U.S. and foreign governments
(4) county departments and the county board
(5) Congress and the president

Think It Through

Which is the correct answer? _____

Why is it correct? Give a specific reason.

_____
_____
_____

Answer and Explanation: The correct answer is **(2) the federal and state governments.** The state government has the authority to regulate the powers of local governments. Similarly, the federal government (through the Constitution) delegates certain powers to the states. Choices (1), (4), and (5) are wrong because they involve a relationship within a single level of government. Choice (3) is incorrect because it involves relationships between sovereign nations.

Practice

Choose the <u>one best answer</u> to the questions below. Write a short explanation for your answers to questions 1 and 2.

<u>Questions 1 and 2</u> are based on this passage.

In South Africa in the early 1900s, many legal restrictions were placed on Indians who had moved there. For example, they could not travel freely throughout the country or buy property. Led by Mohandas Gandhi, Indians used tactics of civil disobedience to force the South African government to change: they held illegal but peaceful protests; they entered areas forbidden to them. Using these nonviolent tactics, Gandhi forced South Africa to ease some of the restrictions on Indians.

1. Which tactic might be used in a campaign of civil disobedience in the United States?

    (1) refusing to pay taxes
    (2) rioting and destroying property
    (3) voting for a candidate
    (4) writing a letter to the editor
    (5) observing legislative sessions

    Answer choice _____

    Explanation _____

2. Which is MOST similar to Gandhi's campaign in South Africa?

    (1) the American Revolution
    (2) the U.S. Civil War
    (3) the British takeover of India
    (4) U.S. participation in the United Nations
    (5) the U.S. Civil Rights movement

    Answer choice _____

    Explanation _____

<u>Questions 3 and 4</u> are based on this passage.

The U.S. Geological Survey produces and sells several types of maps:

Topographic maps—These show the shape and elevation of the land.

Photo-image maps—These use aerial photographs to show detail in areas of low relief, such as coastal zones and farmland.

Geologic maps—These show the composition and structure of Earth's materials.

Hydrologic maps—These show water-related information such as flood plains, irrigated land, and aquifers.

Thematic maps—These show specific information such as population distribution, climate zones, and farm products.

3. Bryanna is interested in mountain climbing in the Adirondack Mountains. Which type of USGS map would be MOST useful for her?

    (1) a topographic map
    (2) a photo-image map
    (3) a geologic map
    (4) a hydrologic map
    (5) a thematic map

4. Shelby wants to prospect for gold in Alaska. Which type of USGS map would be MOST useful for him?

    (1) a topographic map
    (2) a photo-image map
    (3) a geologic map
    (4) a hydrologic map
    (5) a thematic map

Check answers and explanations on page 40.

Analyze What You Read

On the GED Social Studies Test, some questions ask you to **analyze** information, or explore the relationships among ideas. Some questions involve determining cause and effect or drawing conclusions. Others involve analyzing subjective matters: distinguishing facts from opinions, identifying point of view, and recognizing information designed to persuade people.

EXAMPLE

In the early 1790s, the North's booming textile industry needed cotton. Southern planters couldn't meet the demand because the slave labor required to pick seeds from cotton by hand was costly. In 1792, Eli Whitney invented the cotton gin, which made it possible to remove seeds from cotton economically. Planters began to raise more cotton, and the demand for slaves grew. By 1794, the price of a field hand had tripled.

Based on the paragraph, what caused the growth of slavery in the South in the 1790s?

(1) the Northern textile mills' need for workers
(2) the need to clean cotton by hand
(3) the high cost of maintaining slaves
(4) the increase in the Southern cotton crop
(5) the increase in the price of a field hand

Answer and Explanations

(1) Textile workers came from areas near the mills; they were not Southern slaves.
(2) Before the cotton gin, the difficulty of handpicking cottonseeds prevented Southern planters from increasing the amount of cotton grown.
(3) In 1790, the cost of keeping slaves was high compared to the profit that could be made from cotton. This affected the growth of slavery until after 1792, when the cotton gin was invented.
(4) **This is correct. The cotton gin cut the cost of producing cotton and encouraged Southern planters to plant more cotton. Thus, they needed more slaves to raise the cotton.**
(5) The increase in the price of a field hand was a result, not a cause, of the increased need for slaves to raise more cotton.

Try It Yourself

We use coins and paper as money. However, other items, such as cattle, cigarettes, shells, and stones, have also been used as money. What conclusion can you draw from this?

(1) Bartering is easier than using money.
(2) Whatever is accepted as money is money.
(3) Coins and bills are worth more than shells.
(4) Only coins and bills are useful as money.
(5) Coins are valued by metal content.

Think It Through

Which is the correct answer? _____

Why is it correct? Give a specific reason.

_____

_____

_____

Answer and Explanation: The correct answer is **(2) Whatever is accepted as money is money.** Since many things have been used as money, money's value comes from its acceptance as a means of exchange. Choice (1) is wrong because bartering requires that each person want what the other has. Choices (3) and (5) are incorrect because the passage does not give information about the relative values of coins, bills, shells, or metals, which, in any case, depend on the society or culture in which they are being exchanged. Choice (4) is contradicted by the passage.

Practice

Choose the <u>one best answer</u> to the questions below. Write a short explanation for your answers to questions 1 and 2.

<u>Questions 1 and 2</u> are based on this excerpt from a brochure mailed to all state residents.

Bioterrorism is the intentional use of germs to spread illness and fear. Our state is preparing for a possible bioterrorism event by training healthcare workers, vaccinating some healthcare workers against smallpox, and increasing the ability of emergency workers to respond to an attack. You can prepare by stocking food, water, and medicines at home.

1. Why does the brochure describe steps taken by the state?

    (1) to define bioterrorism
    (2) to convince healthcare workers to be vaccinated
    (3) to reassure citizens that the state is working to keep them safe
    (4) to give instructions to citizens
    (5) to provide procedural information for healthcare workers

    Answer choice _____

    Explanation _____
    _____

2. Which is an unstated assumption of the brochure?

    (1) The state will not be targeted.
    (2) The government should do more.
    (3) An attack is certain to happen.
    (4) It is possible to contain an attack.
    (5) It is possible to prevent an attack.

    Answer choice _____

    Explanation _____
    _____

<u>Questions 3 and 4</u> are based on this passage.

Although Canada is an English-speaking country, almost 82% of Quebec residents (Québecois) speak French at home. In fact, French is the official language of Quebec, and there are many laws governing the use of French and English. Language is an emotional issue in Quebec. For example, racecar driver Jacques Villeneuve announced he would open a Montreal nightclub called "Newtown," the English version of his name. This angered some French Canadians, who filed complaints with the "language police." Villeneuve responded by saying that he had lived in Switzerland where people speak three or four languages and don't get angry at one another about which language they use.

3. Which is an opinion rather than a fact?

    (1) Most Québecois speak French.
    (2) French is the official language of Quebec.
    (3) In Canada, the use of French and English is regulated by law.
    (4) *Villeneuve* means "new town" in English.
    (5) Villeneuve should not give his restaurant an English name.

4. How did living in Switzerland affect Villeneuve's attitude toward language?

    (1) He came to favor the use of French.
    (2) He came to favor the use of English.
    (3) He came to appreciate tolerance for the use of different languages.
    (4) He decided that language use should be regulated by law.
    (5) He grew to believe that English should be the only language used in Quebec.

Check answers and explanations on page 40.

Evaluate What You Read

On the GED Social Studies Test, you will be asked to **evaluate** information, or judge whether it is accurate or valid. Some questions ask whether specific information supports a conclusion or a generalization. Others ask you to evaluate different points of view, accounts, or interpretations of the same event. Still others ask about the role played by values and beliefs in decision making.

EXAMPLE

Before a big game, a ticket scalper sells a $50 ticket to a fan for $150. To a police officer, this sale is a crime: the law prohibits the resale of tickets for more than 25% above face value. To an economist, this sale is just supply and demand. The fan is willing to pay extra for a ticket because the ticket office is sold out. The scalper is happy to make a large profit.

According to this account, anti-scalping laws are based on which belief?

The laws are based on the belief that

(1) supply and price are related
(2) the greater the supply of tickets, the higher the price
(3) the smaller the supply of tickets, the higher the price
(4) scalping extorts money from fans, forcing them to pay high prices without any choice
(5) the ticket office keeps its own ticket profits

Answer and Explanations

(1) This is an assumption of the law of supply and demand, but it is not the basis of the anti-scalping law.
(2) The greater the supply of tickets, the lower the price would be, according to the law of supply and demand.
(3) This is an example of the law of supply and demand, but it is not the basis of the anti-scalping law.
(4) **This is correct. Anti-scalping laws are based on the idea that the buyer is being forced to pay a higher price for tickets. However, according to the passage, there is no force involved.**
(5) The ticket office keeps its own profits regardless of whether tickets are later resold by scalpers.

Try It Yourself

Which conclusion is supported by the information given in the passage above?

(1) Scalping is a federal offense.
(2) The resale of tickets is always illegal.
(3) Scalping is profitable when demand is strong.
(4) Scalpers' main goal is to help fans.
(5) Scalping is most profitable when tickets first go on sale.

Think It Through

Which is the correct answer? _____

Why is it correct? Give a specific reason.

_____

_____

_____

Answer and Explanation: The correct answer is **(3) Scalping is profitable when demand is strong.** When demand exceeds supply, prices rise, and scalpers make more money. Choice (1) is wrong because the passage does not indicate whether scalping is regulated by state or federal law. Choice (2) is directly contradicted by the passage. Choices (4) and (5) are both untrue; neither is supported by the passage.

Practice

Choose the <u>one best answer</u> to the questions below. Write a short explanation for your answers to questions 1 and 2.

<u>Questions 1 and 2</u> refer to the passage below.

In the United States, the president can limit the power of the judiciary by issuing pardons. A pardon releases someone from his or her crime's legal consequences. The most famous pardon was given by President Ford to former President Nixon for any offenses he may have committed while in office. President George H. W. Bush pardoned government officials for their role in the Iran-Contra scandal.

1. What was MOST LIKELY the reason each president gave for granting pardons?

    (1) Justice must be impartial.
    (2) Enough time has passed.
    (3) The nation needs to move on.
    (4) Punishing politicians is wrong.
    (5) The judiciary needs to be checked.

    Answer choice _____

    Explanation _____
    _____

2. President Carter gave amnesty to 10,000 men who had moved to Canada to avoid being drafted during the Vietnam War. Which group was MOST LIKELY to be opposed to this pardon?

    (1) the Veterans of Foreign Wars
    (2) the League of Women Voters
    (3) the American Civil Liberties Union
    (4) the National Rifle Association
    (5) the National Wildlife Federation

    Answer choice _____

    Explanation _____
    _____

<u>Question 3</u> is based on the passage below.

The Declaration of Independence explained why the American colonists broke away from Great Britain and fought for their rights, among these, "life, liberty, and the pursuit of happiness." John Adams, one of the leaders of the Revolution, wrote to his wife, "I am surprized at the . . . Greatness of this Revolution."

The British took a different view. British General John Burgoyne wrote that the "present unnatural Rebellion" has led to "the compleatest System of Tyranny [including] Arbitrary Imprisonments, Confiscation of Property, Persecution and Torture."

3. How did Adams's and Burgoyne's attitudes toward the Revolutionary War differ?

    (1) Adams thought everyone had the right to life, liberty, and happiness, and Burgoyne thought only the British did.
    (2) Adams thought the Revolution would result in a great nation, and Burgoyne thought Great Britain would win.
    (3) Adams supported any means to win the Revolution, and Burgoyne disapproved of imprisonment, torture, and other means.
    (4) Adams thought the Revolution could not be justified, and Burgoyne thought it resulted in tyranny.
    (5) Adams had an idealistic view of the Revolution's goals, and Burgoyne had a negative view of its means.

Check answers and explanations on page 40.

Step 3: Practice Social Studies Graphic Skills

Read Timelines, Charts, and Diagrams

On the GED Social Studies Test, you will have to read and interpret social studies information in **timelines, charts, tables,** and **diagrams.**

EXAMPLE

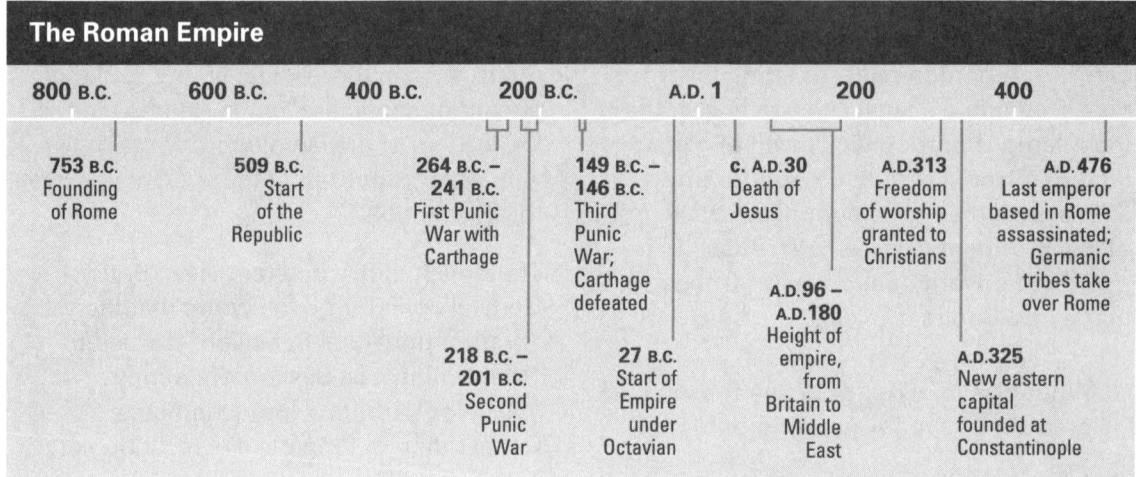

According to the timeline, when did Rome adopt a republican form of government?

(1) in 753 B.C.
(2) in 509 B.C.
(3) in 27 B.C.
(4) in 313
(5) in 476

Answer and Explanations

(1) The city was founded in 753 B.C.
(2) **This is correct. Skim the events of the timeline to find the establishment of the Republic. Then check the year in which this occurred.**
(3) The Roman Empire began in 27 B.C.
(4) Christians were granted freedom of worship in 313.
(5) Rome fell to Germanic tribes in 476.

Try It Yourself

According to the timeline above, which event occurred after the Roman Empire reached its peak?

(1) the First Punic War with Carthage
(2) the Third Punic War with Carthage
(3) Octavian's rule as emperor
(4) the death of Jesus
(5) the establishment of an eastern capital

Think It Through

Which is the correct answer? _____

Why is it correct? Give a specific reason.

_____

_____

_____

Answer and Explanation: The correct answer is **(5) the establishment of an eastern capital.** The Roman Empire peaked from 96 to 180, according to the timeline. Choices (1) through (4) are incorrect because they occurred before 96.

Practice

Choose the <u>one best answer</u> to the questions below. Write a short explanation for your answers to questions 1 and 2.

<u>Questions 1 and 2</u> are based on the table below.

Water Quality by Type of Water Body, 1998			
Type	Good	Good but Threatened	Polluted
Rivers, streams	55%	10%	35%
Lakes, ponds	46%	9%	45%
Estuaries	47%	10%	43%
Great Lakes shores	2%	2%	96%
Ocean shores	80%	8%	12%

Source: Statistical Abstract of the United States

<u>Questions 3 through 5</u> are based on the diagram below.

Structure of the Japanese Government

(Diagram: Prime Minister — Appoints → Cabinet; Emperor; Prime Minister Chooses Cabinet; Can dismiss Diet; Diet contains House of Representatives and House of Councillors; Voters Elect Diet; Diet Chooses Prime Minister)

1. What percentage of estuaries are polluted?

   (1) 10%
   (2) 35%
   (3) 43%
   (4) 47%
   (5) 53%

   Answer choice _____

   Explanation _____
   _____

2. Which habitat has been MOST affected by industrial development?

   (1) rivers and streams
   (2) lakes and ponds
   (3) estuaries
   (4) the shores of the Great Lakes
   (5) the ocean shores

   Answer choice _____

   Explanation _____
   _____

3. How does the prime minister get this job?

   (1) by appointment of the Emperor
   (2) by appointment of the Cabinet
   (3) through selection by the whole Diet
   (4) through selection by the House of Councillors
   (5) by election of the voters

4. To which U.S. government structure is the Diet MOST similar?

   (1) the Cabinet
   (2) the Supreme Court
   (3) the State Department
   (4) the Senate
   (5) Congress

5. Which of the following conclusions is supported by the diagram?

   (1) The Emperor has little real power.
   (2) The Diet is corrupt.
   (3) The prime minister can dissolve the Diet.
   (4) Elections are held at fixed intervals.
   (5) Japan has a two-party system.

Check answers and explanations on page 40.

Read Graphs

On the GED Social Studies Test, you will have to read and interpret the information in **line graphs, bar graphs,** and **circle graphs.** Questions based on graphs may ask you to find data on the graphs. They may also ask you to analyze, apply, or evaluate the data on the graphs.

EXAMPLE

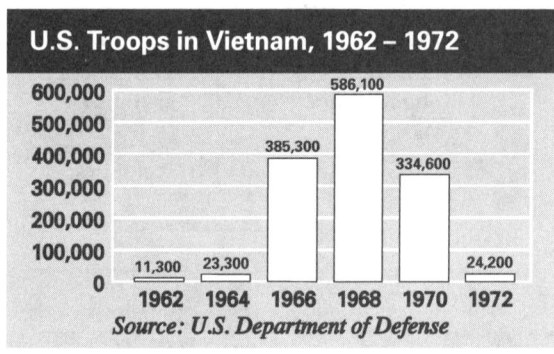

How many U.S. troops were in Vietnam in 1966?

(1) 11,300
(2) 24,200
(3) 334,600
(4) 385,300
(5) 586,100

Answer and Explanations

(1) This is the number of U.S. troops in Vietnam in 1962.
(2) This is the number of U.S. troops in Vietnam in 1972.
(3) This is the number of U.S. troops in Vietnam in 1970.
(4) **This is correct. Locate 1966 on the horizontal axis, and then read the number at the top of the bar. This is the number of U.S. troops in Vietnam in 1966.**
(5) This is the number of U.S. troops in Vietnam in 1968.

Try It Yourself

When Richard Nixon became president in 1969, he promised to shift the war burden to South Vietnam. How does the graph support the conclusion that Nixon kept his promise?

(1) It shows low U.S. troop levels in Vietnam in the early 1960s.
(2) It shows U.S. troop levels rising between 1962 and 1968.
(3) It shows that in 1968, there were 586,100 U.S. troops in Vietnam.
(4) It shows troop levels were similar in 1966 and 1970.
(5) It shows that between 1970 and 1972, over 300,000 U.S. troops left Vietnam.

Think It Through

Which is the correct answer? _____

Why is it correct? Give a specific reason.

_____
_____
_____

Answer and Explanation: The correct answer is **(5) It shows that between 1970 and 1972, over 300,000 U.S. troops left Vietnam.** Nixon made his promise in 1969. That he was able to withdraw huge numbers of soldiers from Vietnam is evidence that he did shift the burden of fighting the war to the South Vietnamese. Choices (1) through (3) are incorrect because they involve data from before Nixon became president. Choice (4) is wrong because the similarity does not indicate a reduction in troops during Nixon's term.

Practice

Choose the <u>one best answer</u> to the questions below. Write a short explanation for your answers to questions 1 and 2.

Questions 1 and 2 are based on the line graph below.

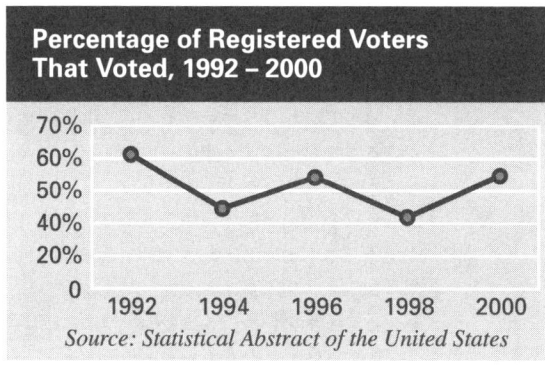
Source: Statistical Abstract of the United States

1. In which year was voter turnout highest?

   (1) 1992
   (2) 1994
   (3) 1996
   (4) 1998
   (5) 2000

   Answer choice _____

   Explanation _____

2. Voter turnout is usually highest during years with presidential elections. Based on this information and the graph, in which years would you conclude presidential elections were held?

   (1) 1992, 1994, and 1996
   (2) 1992, 1996, and 2000
   (3) 1994 and 1998
   (4) 1994, 1996, and 1998
   (5) 1996, 1998, and 2000

   Answer choice _____

   Explanation _____

Questions 3 and 4 are based on the circle graph below.

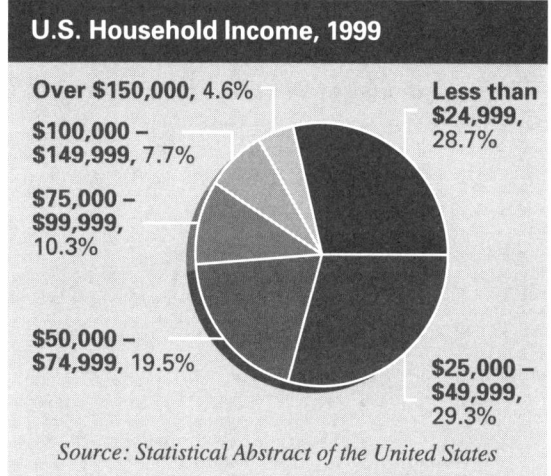
Source: Statistical Abstract of the United States

3. In 1999, what percentage of U.S. households had an annual income between $50,000 and $74,999?

   (1) 29.3%
   (2) 28.7%
   (3) 19.5%
   (4) 10.3%
   (5) 7.7%

4. Which of the following conclusions about U.S. household income in 1999 is supported by the data in the graph?

   (1) The median household income was $41,994.
   (2) The larger a household, the higher its income.
   (3) Households headed by men had higher incomes than those headed by women.
   (4) Almost 10% of households had an income over $150,000.
   (5) Almost 60% of U.S. households had an income less than $50,000.

Check answers and explanations on page 41.

Read Editorial Cartoons and Photos

On the GED Test, you will have to answer questions based on **editorial cartoons** and **photos**.

EXAMPLE

Chris Madden

What is the main idea of this cartoon?

(1) Tuna and cod are the best-selling fish.
(2) Tuna and cod are healthy foods to eat.
(3) If fishing trends continue, tuna and cod soon will be endangered.
(4) Ocean resources are dwindling.
(5) Restaurants should not serve endangered species of fish.

Answer and Explanations

(1) The cartoon does not indicate anything about the popularity of tuna and cod compared with other fish.
(2) Nothing in the cartoon indicates that the cartoonist is promoting the nutritional value of these fish.
(3) **This is correct. Tuna and cod are not actually on the endangered species list. The cartoonist is using this restaurant name to make the point that if present trends continue, these fish may soon be endangered.**
(4) This choice is too broad. Fish are just one resource found in the ocean. We also get different types of seafood and some minerals from the oceans.
(5) It is illegal for restaurants to serve endangered species of any animal or plant. But nothing in the cartoon indicates that this is the main idea. Instead, the cartoonist is using the idea of an endangered species restaurant to make a point.

Try It Yourself

Which action would the cartoonist support?

(1) banning fish in restaurants
(2) lowering the price of tuna and cod
(3) importing fish from foreign countries
(4) limiting commercial fishing of tuna and cod
(5) closing down fish farms

Think It Through

Which is the correct answer? _____

Why is it correct? Give a specific reason.

_____

_____

Answer and Explanation: The correct answer is **(4) limiting commercial fishing of tuna and cod.** The cartoonist is concerned about the decline in food fish, so he would favor measures to allow the fish populations to recover. Choice (1) is too extreme an action. Choice (2) would increase the demand for these fish. Choice (3) means the continued decline of fish populations elsewhere. Choice (5) does not affect the population of fish in the ocean.

Practice

Choose the <u>one best answer</u> to the questions below. Write a short explanation for your answers to questions 1 and 2.

Questions 1 and 2 are based on the cartoon.

Kirk Walters 11/02

1. What does the seesaw represent?

   (1) the executive branch of government
   (2) the judicial branch of government
   (3) the legislative branch of government
   (4) the state court system
   (5) the voters

   Answer choice _____

   Explanation _____
   _____

2. What caused the shift in the balance of power?

   (1) The Republicans won many of the midterm elections.
   (2) The Democrats won many of the midterm elections.
   (3) The media favored the Republicans.
   (4) The media favored the Democrats.
   (5) The number of Democrats increased.

   Answer choice _____

   Explanation _____
   _____

Questions 3 and 4 are based on the following information and photograph.

In 1869, Wyoming was the first state to grant women the right to vote. The photo below shows a women's suffrage parade in 1911.

Culver Pictures

3. What can be inferred from the information and the photo?

   (1) Most men supported the suffragists.
   (2) The suffragists used many tactics.
   (3) Women took over politics in Wyoming.
   (4) In 1911, women in New York still did not have the right to vote.
   (5) Women were denied the vote for the same reasons that criminals were.

4. In 1920, the Nineteenth Amendment to the Constitution granted women the right to vote. What happened as a result?

   (1) Some state voting laws became unconstitutional.
   (2) Women regardless of age could vote.
   (3) Suffragists joined temperance groups.
   (4) More people joined the suffragists.
   (5) Voter turnout decreased overall.

Check answers and explanations on page 41.

Read Maps

Some of the questions on the GED Social Studies Test are based on **maps.** Maps often have titles and a key to symbols that can help you interpret them.

EXAMPLE

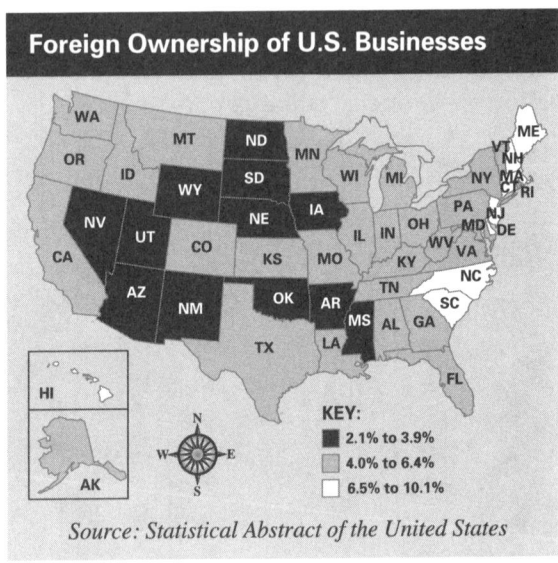

Which of these states has foreign business ownership in the 6.5% to 10.1% range?

(1) Arizona
(2) Illinois
(3) North Carolina
(4) Pennsylvania
(5) Wisconsin

Answer and Explanations

(1) Arizona has foreign business ownership in the 2.1% to 3.9% range.
(2) Illinois has foreign business ownership in the 4.0% to 6.4% range.
(3) **This is correct. Look at the map key to see how states in the 6.5% to 10.1% range are shown. They are white. Of the states listed, only North Carolina is white. Thus, North Carolina has foreign business ownership in that percentage range.**
(4) Pennsylvania has foreign business ownership in the 4.0% to 6.4% range.
(5) Wisconsin has foreign business ownership in the 4.0% to 6.4% range.

Try It Yourself

Which generalization is supported by the map?

(1) The greatest percentage of foreign business ownership is on the West Coast.
(2) The smallest percentage of foreign business ownership is in inland states.
(3) Foreign business ownership is European.
(4) Foreign business ownership is increasing.
(5) Foreign business ownership is decreasing.

Think It Through

Which is the correct answer? _____

Why is it correct? Give a specific reason.

_____
_____
_____

Answer and Explanation: The correct answer is **(2) The smallest percentage of foreign business ownership is in inland states.** Only one of the states in the lowest percentage range (Mississippi) is a coastal state. Choice (1) is wrong because the greatest concentration is on the East Coast. Choices (3) through (5) are not supported by any data on the map.

Practice

Choose the <u>one best answer</u> to the questions below. Write a short explanation for your answers to questions 1 and 2.

<u>Questions 1 and 2</u> are based on this map.

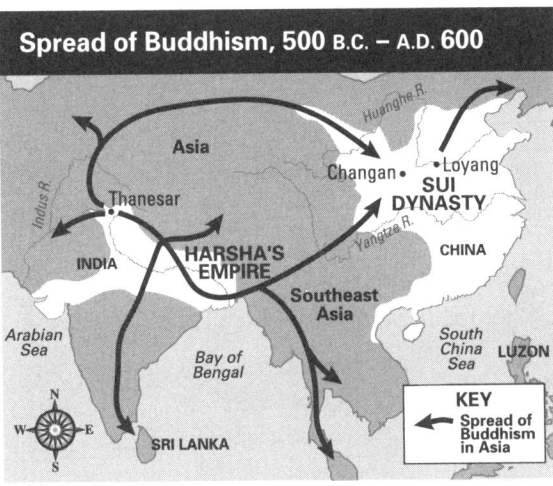

<u>Questions 3 and 4</u> are based on this map.

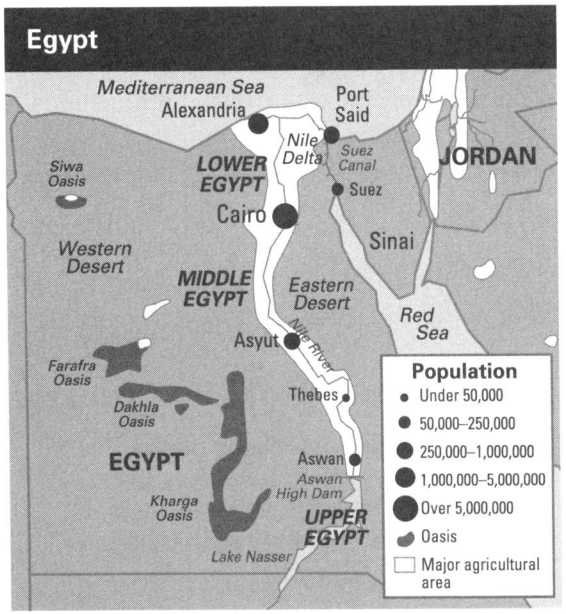

1. Where did Buddhism originate?

   (1) in northern India
   (2) in southern India
   (3) in Southeast Asia
   (4) in China
   (5) in Luzon

   Answer choice _____

   Explanation _____

2. Which information supports the conclusion that MOST travel was over land before 600?

   (1) Buddhism spread to Luzon.
   (2) Buddhism spread on Asia's mainland.
   (3) India was far from China.
   (4) Buddhism crossed the Bay of Bengal.
   (5) Southern Asia has many islands.

   Answer choice _____

   Explanation _____

3. Which city has a population under 50,000?

   (1) Alexandria
   (2) Cairo
   (3) Asyut
   (4) Thebes
   (5) Port Said

4. Where would you conclude that MOST people in Egypt live?

   (1) in the Western Desert
   (2) in Upper Egypt
   (3) along the Nile River
   (4) in the oases
   (5) along the Red Sea

   Check answers and explanations on page 41.

Step 4: Practice Taking the GED

Determine Your Test-Taking Style

On pages 25–37, you will take a full-length practice test to help you get ready for the actual GED Test. Before you take the practice test, look at two approaches to answering test questions.

Test-Taking Style 1: Some people preview the passages and graphics and the question stems (but not the answer choices) first. This gives them an idea of what to look for when they go back to carefully read the passage and answer the questions. Previewing takes only 20 or 30 seconds and helps some people get oriented to the material.

Test-Taking Style 2: Other people prefer to read a passage or graphic thoroughly. Then they go on to answer the questions, referring back to the passage or graphic as necessary.

Try both styles to see which one works best for you. Now is the time to experiment to find out your preferred test-taking style. The hints below will help you, no matter which style you choose.

Test-Taking Style 1: Preview, Read, and Answer

<u>Questions 1 and 2</u> are based on the information and the diagram below.

The Constitution provides a process for changing itself, as shown in this diagram:

Amendment proposed by	Amendment ratified by
Congress: by 2/3 vote of each house	Legislatures of 3/4 of states
or	or
National convention asked for by 2/3 of states	Special conventions in 3/4 of states

> Read the direction line. Note that two questions will refer to this information and diagram. Always read the directions carefully so that you'll know what the questions are based on.

> Skim the information and preview the diagram. Read the title, if any, and the labels. Ask yourself, *What is the main idea of the information and the diagram?*

1. What is the BEST title for this material?

    (1) The Constitution
    (2) Constitutional Conventions
    (3) All of Our Constitutional Amendments
    (4) Ratification of Amendments
    (5) The Amendment Process

> Now, read the question stems—the numbered part. Do not read the answer choices yet. Just keep the questions in mind.

2. What is an unstated assumption of the framers of the amendment provision?

    (1) Congress will never get a 2/3 vote.
    (2) Legislatures will never get a 3/4 vote.
    (3) Conventions are better than legislatures.
    (4) The Constitution should be hard to amend.
    (5) Power to amend should reside with the federal government.

> When you have finished previewing, go back to the information and the diagram. This time, read the information carefully and interpret the diagram. Then answer the two questions.

Test-Taking Style 2: Read, Review, and Answer

Questions 3 and 4 are based on the passage and the map below.

Under President Theodore Roosevelt, the United States began policing the Western Hemisphere. The map shows some interventions in the Caribbean.

Always read the directions carefully so that you'll know what the questions are based on. Note that two questions will refer to this passage and map.

Read the passage. Interpret the map.

3. Which nation did the United States occupy from 1915 to 1934?

   (1) Honduras
   (2) Nicaragua
   (3) Dominican Republic
   (4) Haiti
   (5) Jamaica

Now, answer the first question. Notice that to answer this question, you have to look back at the map only, not at the passage.

4. To what is this foreign policy MOST similar?

   (1) U.S. occupation of Afghanistan and Iraq
   (2) the embargo on trade with Cuba
   (3) U.S. participation in the World Bank
   (4) the negotiation of trade treaties
   (5) the use of foreign aid in diplomacy

Now, answer the second question. To answer this question, you have to review both the passage and the map.

Check answers and explanations on page 41.

Test-Taking Style Self-Evaluation

☐ I felt better first previewing the material and then going back to read and answer the questions. (Style 1)

☐ I felt better plunging into the material, reading carefully, and answering the questions. (Style 2)

☐ I will try Style ____ on the Warm-Up on pages 22–23. If it doesn't work for me, I will change my style.

Practice Test Warm-Up Exercise

Answer the questions below. Explain why you chose the answers that you did. Check your answers and review the explanations on page 23.

<u>Questions 1 and 2</u> are based on this passage.

In 1948, McDonald's method of doing business was unique for a restaurant. By limiting its menu to hamburgers and a few other items, McDonald's reduced waste. It also raised worker productivity through specialization. Each McDonald's restaurant had a fry specialist, a grill specialist, and a shakes specialist. Operations in all restaurants were standardized through training programs for restaurant owners, managers, and employees.

1. To what is McDonald's specialization of food production jobs most similar?

   (1) unpaid summer internships
   (2) a custom furniture maker's workshop
   (3) the jobs on a factory assembly line
   (4) a management training program
   (5) a doctor's specialization in pediatrics

   Answer choice _____

   Explanation _____
   _____

2. From a consumer's point of view, what are advantages of the type of specialization that a restaurant like McDonald's offers?

   (1) low wages but flexible hours
   (2) predictable food at low prices
   (3) unique menus and local color
   (4) standardized production techniques
   (5) high worker productivity

   Answer choice _____

   Explanation _____
   _____

<u>Questions 3 and 4</u> are based on this graph.

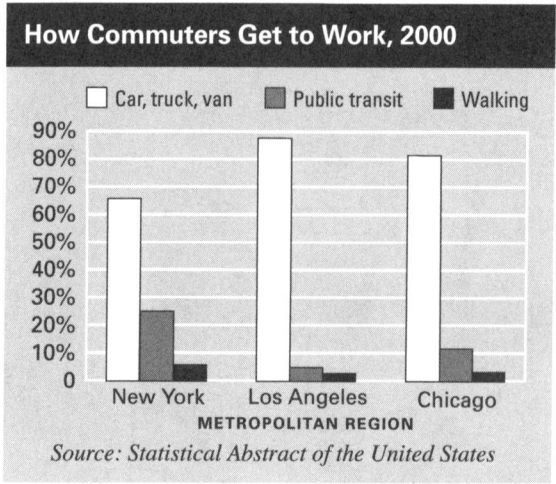

Source: Statistical Abstract of the United States

3. What percentage of workers in New York commute by train, bus, or subway?

   (1) 6%
   (2) 25%
   (3) 65%
   (4) 80%
   (5) almost 90%

   Answer choice _____

   Explanation _____
   _____

4. What conclusion about commuting in U.S. cities is supported by the graph?

   (1) Public transit is growing in U.S. cities.
   (2) Commuters prefer walking to work.
   (3) People prefer commuting by car.
   (4) The average commute is 31 minutes.
   (5) Many people commute to the suburbs.

   Answer choice _____

   Explanation _____
   _____

Warm-Up Answers and Explanations

Check your answers and read the explanations. Then evaluate how well you did.

1. **(3) the jobs on a factory assembly line**

   Explanation: This **application** question asks you to pick out a method of organizing work similar to the way McDonald's organized restaurant food production. A factory assembly line works on the same principle—limited, repeated tasks for each worker to cut training costs and increase productivity.

   Choice (1) is incorrect because there is no particular work method associated with internships and because the work is unpaid.

   Choice (2) is incorrect because a custom furniture maker does not standardize and divide up tasks, but adapts them to suit each unique order.

   Choice (4) is incorrect because management trainees are taught a little bit about everything in a company.

   Choice (5) is incorrect because a pediatrician's work is not divided into tasks to be done by many people.

2. **(2) predictable food at low prices**

   Explanation: This **analysis** question asks you to consider the benefits to the consumer of McDonald's approach to running a restaurant. Since consumers value low price and consistent quality, these are the advantages of specialization that they consider important.

   Choice (1) is incorrect because these are factors that employees, not consumers, generally consider.

   Choice (3) is incorrect because the McDonald's menu was standardized across the nation.

   Choices (4) and (5) are incorrect because restaurant managers, not consumers, care about production techniques and worker productivity.

3. **(2) 25%**

   Explanation: This **comprehension** question asks you to find the percentage of New York area workers who commute by public transit. Find New York on the horizontal axis. Look at the key to see which bar represents public transit. It is the bar that is shaded a medium green. This bar shows about 25%.

   Choice (1) is incorrect because 6% is the percentage of commuters who walk to work in New York.

   Choice (3) is incorrect because 65% is the percentage of commuters who drive to work in New York.

   Choice (4) is incorrect because 80% is the percentage of commuters who drive to work in Chicago.

   Choice (5) is incorrect because almost 90% is the approximate percentage of commuters who drive to work in Los Angeles.

4. **(3) People prefer commuting by car.**

   Explanation: This **evaluation** question asks you to determine which conclusion is supported by the graph. The graph shows that an overwhelming majority of commuters drive to work in each of the three cities listed. This is strong evidence that driving is the preferred method of commuting in U.S. cities.

   Choice (1) is incorrect because the graph gives no information that could be used to draw conclusions about the growth of public transit over time.

   Choice (2) is incorrect because there are few walkers in all three metropolitan areas.

   Choices (4) and (5) are incorrect because the graph gives no information that could be used to draw conclusions about average commuting time or about the geographic distribution of jobs in metropolitan areas.

Warm-Up Self-Evaluation

Question 1 ☐ Correct ☐ Incorrect   Question 3 ☐ Correct ☐ Incorrect
Question 2 ☐ Correct ☐ Incorrect   Question 4 ☐ Correct ☐ Incorrect

When I take the Practice GED Social Studies Test, I need to be careful to:

_____

_____

Strategies for Passing the GED Social Studies Test

1. **Always follow test instructions.** Listen to any instructions the test provider gives you, and read the instructions at the beginning of the test and at the beginning of item sets. Don't just dive in!

2. **Pace yourself.** You have 70 minutes to answer 50 questions—a little over a minute per question. If you find yourself staring at the same question for five minutes, you are wasting time. Make your best guess and move on. You can recheck difficult questions after you finish the test.

   Don't expect to spend the same amount of time on each question. Instead, check your progress at regular intervals. For example, after working for 15 minutes on a 70-minute GED Social Studies Test, you should have answered 10 or 11 questions. If you are making faster progress, that's fine. If you are progressing too slowly, pick up the pace.

   If you generally have trouble pacing yourself on tests, practice your pacing on a couple of short tests. Use a watch or stopwatch to time yourself. Check your progress at regular intervals, and speed up if necessary. The more tests you take, the better your pacing will be.

3. **Read passages carefully, and find the main idea.** Take time to read each passage carefully—more than once if you need to in order to understand it. If an event is described, try to "picture it" in your mind as you read. If the passage is a quotation from a historic document, think about the historical period and the document's significance. If the passage is from a practical document, focus on its purpose. Refer back to the passage for details when you are answering the questions.

4. **Use titles and labels to help you interpret graphics.** The graphics in the Social Studies Test "show" rather than "tell." It is often a good idea to preview the graphics, reading the titles and the main labels. Then read any additional information provided, such as a definition or passage. When you answer the questions, you may need to find details in the graphic or interpret its meaning. You may also need to draw on information from both the graphic and the text that accompanies it. Go back and look for the specific information you need to answer each question.

5. **Predict the answer when you read a question.** If you can answer a question in your mind, do so, and then look for your answer as you read all of the choices. However, make sure to always read all of the answer choices. Even if you feel sure that the first choice is the correct one, you need to check all of the choices to make sure.

6. **If you get stuck on a question, take a guess.** First eliminate any answer choices you think are wrong. Then make a good guess from among the remaining choices. Since there is no penalty for wrong answers on the GED, it's better to guess than to skip a question. If you are entirely blocked on a question, make a quick guess, put a light mark next to the question line on your answer sheet, and go on. You can return to the question at the end of the testing period if you have time. Then you might be able to figure out the answer or improve your guess.

7. **Check periodically to make sure that you are marking the answer sheet properly.** If you are answering question 9, make sure you are marking line 9 on the answer sheet. *This is particularly important if you decide to skip a question.* Skipping questions is not recommended, but if you do skip a question, make sure to skip the corresponding numbered line on the answer sheet, as well. Fill in only one answer for each question. If you decide to change an answer to a question, erase the original answer thoroughly. Finally, when you are finished with the test, be sure to erase any stray marks on your answer sheet.

Practice GED Social Studies Test

Directions

This *Practice GED Social Studies Test* is similar to an actual GED Test. The test consists of multiple-choice questions intended to assess your understanding of history, civics and government, economics, and geography. The questions are based on short readings or graphics—including timelines, charts, tables, graphs, maps, editorial cartoons, and photographs.

Read each passage, study the graphics, and then answer the questions. You may refer back to the passage or graphic at any time.

You will have 70 minutes to answer 50 questions. Work carefully, but do not spend too much time on any one question. Be sure to answer every question. You may copy and use the answer sheet below, or you may write your answers on another sheet of paper.

After you have finished, check the practice test answers and explanations on pages 41–44. Enter your scores in the evaluation chart on page 38. You and your teacher will use the results of this test to complete the Personal Study Planner on page 39.

You may begin now.

1. ① ② ③ ④ ⑤	11. ① ② ③ ④ ⑤	21. ① ② ③ ④ ⑤	31. ① ② ③ ④ ⑤	41. ① ② ③ ④ ⑤
2. ① ② ③ ④ ⑤	12. ① ② ③ ④ ⑤	22. ① ② ③ ④ ⑤	32. ① ② ③ ④ ⑤	42. ① ② ③ ④ ⑤
3. ① ② ③ ④ ⑤	13. ① ② ③ ④ ⑤	23. ① ② ③ ④ ⑤	33. ① ② ③ ④ ⑤	43. ① ② ③ ④ ⑤
4. ① ② ③ ④ ⑤	14. ① ② ③ ④ ⑤	24. ① ② ③ ④ ⑤	34. ① ② ③ ④ ⑤	44. ① ② ③ ④ ⑤
5. ① ② ③ ④ ⑤	15. ① ② ③ ④ ⑤	25. ① ② ③ ④ ⑤	35. ① ② ③ ④ ⑤	45. ① ② ③ ④ ⑤
6. ① ② ③ ④ ⑤	16. ① ② ③ ④ ⑤	26. ① ② ③ ④ ⑤	36. ① ② ③ ④ ⑤	46. ① ② ③ ④ ⑤
7. ① ② ③ ④ ⑤	17. ① ② ③ ④ ⑤	27. ① ② ③ ④ ⑤	37. ① ② ③ ④ ⑤	47. ① ② ③ ④ ⑤
8. ① ② ③ ④ ⑤	18. ① ② ③ ④ ⑤	28. ① ② ③ ④ ⑤	38. ① ② ③ ④ ⑤	48. ① ② ③ ④ ⑤
9. ① ② ③ ④ ⑤	19. ① ② ③ ④ ⑤	29. ① ② ③ ④ ⑤	39. ① ② ③ ④ ⑤	49. ① ② ③ ④ ⑤
10. ① ② ③ ④ ⑤	20. ① ② ③ ④ ⑤	30. ① ② ③ ④ ⑤	40. ① ② ③ ④ ⑤	50. ① ② ③ ④ ⑤

This page may be photocopied for classroom use.

Choose the one best answer to the questions below.

Questions 1 and 2 refer to the passage below.

Christopher Columbus recorded his observations of the New World in a diary that he kept for Queen Isabella of Spain. The entry for October 13, 1492, reads in part:

". . . [The people] have so little to give but will give it all for whatever we give them. . . . One seaman gave [less than a penny] for about 25 pounds of spun cotton. I probably should have forbidden this exchange, but I wanted to take the cotton to Your Highnesses. . . . I think the cotton is grown on San Salvador, but I cannot say for sure because I have not been here that long. Also, the gold they wear . . . comes from here, but in order not to lose time I want to go and see if I can find the island of Japan."

1. Based on the quote, what do you infer is the reason Columbus thought he should have stopped the sailor's purchase of cotton?

    (1) The cotton was of poor quality.
    (2) There was no room for cotton on his ships.
    (3) The seaman did not need so much cotton.
    (4) The transaction was unfair to the island people.
    (5) Spain had plenty of its own cotton.

2. Based on the quote, which of the following did Columbus assume to be true?

    (1) Cotton was of little value to Isabella.
    (2) The natives of San Salvador were good warriors.
    (3) He had plenty of time to explore San Salvador.
    (4) San Salvador was near an unknown continent.
    (5) He had almost achieved his goal of reaching eastern Asia.

Questions 3 and 4 refer to the chart below.

Career Experience of Recent Presidents

President	Occupation	Last Office Held Before the Presidency	Age When Assumed Presidency
Jimmy Carter	Business owner (farmer)	Governor of Georgia	52
Ronald Reagan	Actor	Governor of California	69
George H.W. Bush	Business owner	Vice president	64
Bill Clinton	Lawyer	Governor of Arkansas	46
George W. Bush	Business owner	Governor of Texas	54

3. Of the presidents listed, who was the youngest at the time of his inauguration?

    (1) Jimmy Carter
    (2) Ronald Reagan
    (3) George H. W. Bush
    (4) Bill Clinton
    (5) George W. Bush

4. Which of the following people is MOST likely to make practical use of the information in this chart?

    (1) an undecided voter during a presidential election year
    (2) an ambitious, young politician planning his or her political career
    (3) the head of a special-interest lobbying group
    (4) a member of the U.S. House of Representatives
    (5) a volunteer in the campaign of a presidential candidate

Questions 5 and 6 refer to the graph below.

Fast-Growing Occupations, 2000 – 2010

Education/Training Required:
☐ On-the-job training ■ Associate's degree
■ Bachelor's degree

- Food preparers and servers
- Customer service representatives
- Registered nurses
- Retail salespersons
- Computer support specialists
- General and operations managers

0 300 400 500 600 700
PROJECTED NUMBER OF NEW JOBS (IN THOUSANDS)

Source: Bureau of Labor Statistics

5. Which of the following occupations requires the minimum training of an associate's degree?

   (1) food preparer and server
   (2) customer service representative
   (3) retail salesperson
   (4) computer support specialist
   (5) general and operations manager

6. On the basis of this graph, Lester decides that being a food preparer or server offers the most economic security. What is wrong with Lester's thinking?

   (1) Almost 700,000 new jobs for food servers and preparers will open up between 2000 and 2010.
   (2) Food workers are needed in all parts of the country.
   (3) Jobs with no educational requirements usually do not pay well or offer good opportunities for advancement.
   (4) Food industry jobs will be hard to find.
   (5) Over the course of the decade, the entire job market will grow.

7. In China, each couple is permitted to have only one child. The government advertises this policy in many ways, including using billboards such as the one shown below.

Owen Franken/Stock Boston

How is this billboard designed to persuade Chinese couples to comply with the "one couple, one child" policy?

   (1) by showing a couple with a daughter
   (2) by showing how happy and healthy a couple with one child is
   (3) by explaining how to limit the number of children a couple has
   (4) by convincing couples to take their children for regular doctor visits
   (5) by warning about overpopulation

8. In the 1600s, tulips became highly prized by the Dutch. Demand grew so great during "tulip mania" that the value of tulip bulbs grew by 3000% in just three years. Many people speculated in tulips. Just a few years later, however, the value of tulip investments fell very sharply.

   Which is MOST similar to "tulip mania"?

   (1) the antitrust movement of the 1890s
   (2) the Great Depression of the 1930s
   (3) the New Deal of the 1930s
   (4) the civil rights movement of the 1960s
   (5) the Internet stock boom and bust of the 1990s

9. Many people living in the United States were born in other countries. The graph below shows percentages of foreign-born residents by country for the year 2000.

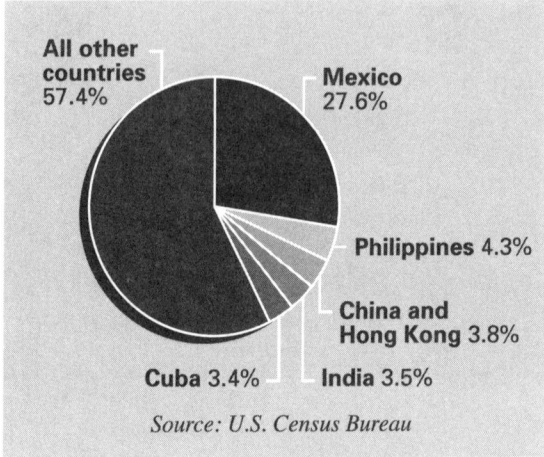
Source: U.S. Census Bureau

What can you conclude from this graph?

(1) Most Mexican residents live in California.
(2) Indian residents outnumber Chinese residents in the United States.
(3) Asians, including Philippinos, Chinese, and Indians, are a growing segment of the foreign-born population.
(4) Most foreign-born residents become citizens within a few years.
(5) Mexicans and Cubans account for about one-third of foreign-born residents.

10. Consumer goods are things that people buy and use directly, such as pens and combs. Capital goods are tools, machinery, and equipment that are used to produce other goods.

Which item is an example of a capital good?

(1) a printing press
(2) a sports car
(3) a pair of pants
(4) a loaf of bread
(5) a video game

Question 11 refers to the passage below.

During the Paleolithic Age, up to about 9000 B.C., all humans lived in small kin groups. They made tools and weapons, such as drills, blades, and arrowheads, from stone and bones. Some of these were highly decorated. They gathered food, since agriculture had not yet been developed. Men hunted and fished, and women picked edible plants, fruits, and nuts. Women also processed animal hides and carved wood to make household objects. Paleolithic artists painted realistic images of game animals such as bison and reindeer on the walls of caves.

Paleolithic culture survived in isolated areas into modern times. For example, some native peoples of the Amazon rainforest still lived like our Paleolithic ancestors when anthropologists first contacted and studied them.

11. Which of the following would provide the BEST evidence that labor was divided by gender during the Paleolithic Age?

(1) edible wild plants
(2) stone and bone tools
(3) abstract designs on weapons
(4) observations of Paleolithic groups that survived into modern times
(5) cave paintings of bison, reindeer, and other game animals

12. The infrastructure of a region or nation consists of the basic foundations of its society: urban centers, transportation networks, mines, energy distribution systems, and facilities such as hospitals and schools.

Which of the following is part of the infrastructure of the United States?

(1) fast food restaurant chains
(2) the Appalachian Mountains
(3) the interstate highway system
(4) the Missouri River
(5) the Mall of America

Questions 13 and 14 refer to the graph below.

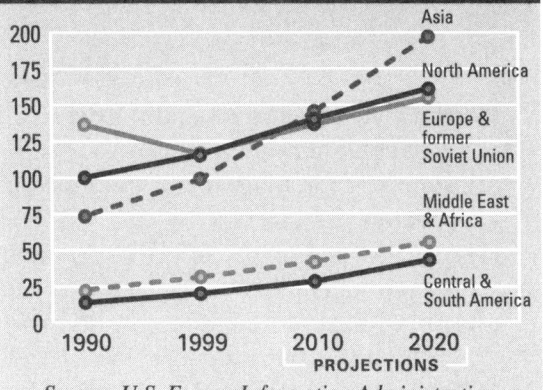

Source: U.S. Energy Information Administration

13. Which region will have the highest energy consumption by 2020?

    (1) North America
    (2) Europe and the former Soviet Union
    (3) Asia
    (4) Middle East and Africa
    (5) Central and South America

14. As a result of the breakup of the Soviet Union, industrial production in that region declined during the 1990s. Which data from the graph supports the conclusion that industrial production is related to energy use?

    Energy use in Europe and the former Soviet Union

    (1) was the highest in the world in 1990
    (2) declined by about 20 quadrillion BTUs between 1990 and 1999
    (3) is projected to increase by about 20 quadrillion BTUs between 1999 and 2010
    (4) is projected to rise steadily until 2020
    (5) is projected to be more than three times higher than that of Central and South America in 2020

Questions 15 through 17 refer to the passage below.

If a senator dies, the U.S. Constitution permits his or her state to appoint a new senator to finish the term. However, the Constitution has no similar provision for the death of a member of the House of Representatives. Instead, an election must be held, and holding an election can take months. Some lawmakers think the Constitution should be amended to allow for the immediate appointment of representatives. They say that a terrorist attack on the Capitol might kill so many representatives that the House would be unable to function when it most needs to.

15. Which of the following is an opinion?

    (1) The Constitution specifies how to replace members of Congress.
    (2) If a senator dies, a new senator can be appointed to the empty seat.
    (3) There is no provision for the appointment of a U.S. representative in case of death of a House member.
    (4) If a member of the House dies, an election must be held to fill the seat.
    (5) The Constitution should be amended to allow appointments to the House in case of the death of representatives.

16. Which values are supporters of this amendment trying to uphold?

    (1) law and order
    (2) life and liberty
    (3) health and wealth
    (4) family values
    (5) economic interdependence

17. What is a good title for this passage?

    (1) Ensuring a Working House of Representatives
    (2) Amending the U.S. Constitution
    (3) Filling a Vacant Senate Seat
    (4) Rules for Senate Elections
    (5) Preventing Future Attacks on the Capitol

18. In the Treaty of Versailles that concluded World War I, the Allies blamed Germany for "all the loss and damage . . . as a consequence of the war." As a result, Germany was made to pay punitive reparations to the Allies.

What was a likely result of these terms?

(1) payment by the Allies for all war damages
(2) resentment in Germany over harsh treatment
(3) inclusion of Germany in the League of Nations
(4) an even balance of power between Germany and the Allies
(5) economic prosperity in Europe

19. In Carver City, the city council must cut expenses in order to balance the city budget. The mayor has suggested cutting the school crossing guards, who cost the city almost $500,000 per year in salary and benefits. According to the mayor, the crossing guards are a luxury that the city can no longer afford. He proposes that parents, teachers, and school janitors serve as crossing guards instead. A group of parents opposes this proposed cut, arguing that the crossing guards are needed to ensure their children's safety.

Which of the following is an opinion?

(1) Carver City is debating how to balance the city's budget.
(2) The budget can be balanced by cutting expenses.
(3) The school crossing guards cost the city almost $500,000 a year.
(4) The school crossing guards are a luxury.
(5) A group of parents opposes the plan to cut the crossing guards.

20. Demand for a product must be backed up by the ability to pay for it. This is sometimes called effective demand. Unless people can pay for a product, the demand for that product does not exist.

What can you conclude about effective demand?

(1) Effective demand does not exist at all in developing nations.
(2) Supply is the main factor influencing effective demand.
(3) As salaries rise, the effective demand for products falls.
(4) During a recession, effective demand for luxury products decreases.
(5) The effective demand for food rises sharply with increases in income.

Question 21 refers to the following graph.

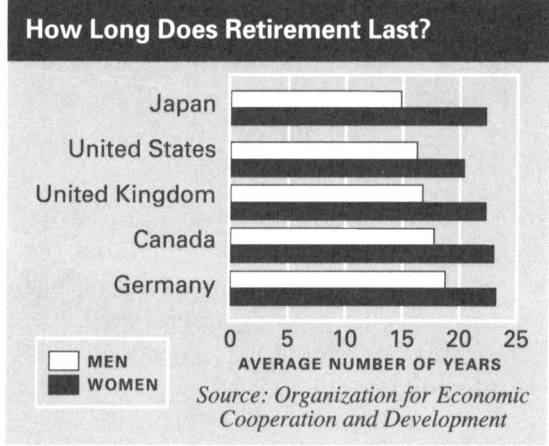

21. Which generalization is supported by the graph?

(1) Women are healthier than men.
(2) Men retire earlier than women.
(3) Women spend more years in retirement than men.
(4) Both men and women retire earlier in Japan than in Germany.
(5) In the United States, retirement tends to last longer than in other nations.

Questions 22 through 25 refer to the following information and map.

From 1791 to 1820, Congress tried to maintain a numerical balance between the free states of the North and the slave states of the South. However, population in the North grew more rapidly. By 1818, the northern states had a majority in the House of Representatives. The Senate was still evenly divided between free states and slave states.

In 1819, Missouri Territory's petition for statehood as a slave state threatened to upset the balance. The Northern states feared losing power to slaveowners' interests. They proposed conditions for Missouri's admission: banning further imports of slaves to Missouri and requiring that all slaves be freed when they turned 25. Outraged, Southerners defeated this proposal in the Senate.

After months of angry debate, Congress passed a plan known as the Missouri Compromise. It admitted Missouri as a slave state and Maine as a free state. It also banned slavery in the territory north of latitude 36°30'. After the Missouri Compromise, the United States looked like this:

22. In which of the following states was slavery legal in 1821?

    (1) Maryland
    (2) Pennsylvania
    (3) Ohio
    (4) Illinois
    (5) Indiana

23. To which split is the 1820 sectional division on slavery MOST similar?

    It is similar to the division between

    (1) the colonies and England in 1776, divided by views on government
    (2) North and South Vietnam in the 1960s, divided by economic and political differences
    (3) "hawks" and "doves" in the 1960s, divided by views on the Vietnam War
    (4) suffragists and their opponents, divided by views on women voting
    (5) isolationists and their opponents, divided by views on foreign affairs

24. What evidence from the passage and map supports the conclusion that the Missouri Compromise maintained the balance between free states and slave states?

    (1) Kentucky was a slave state.
    (2) Arkansas remained open to slavery.
    (3) Florida remained open to slavery.
    (4) The unorganized territory in the upper Midwest was closed to slavery.
    (5) There were 12 free states and 12 slave states.

25. Which was a likely result of the Missouri Compromise?

    (1) It increased regional, not national, loyalty.
    (2) Overall, it weakened the nation's economy.
    (3) It led to population increases in the North.
    (4) It increased the power of the North.
    (5) It increased the power of Congress.

Questions 26 and 27 refer to the information below.

The U.S. Declaration of Independence lists more than 25 actions taken by the king of Great Britain that harmed the American colonies. Here are three of those actions:

"He has refused his assent to laws, the most wholesome and necessary for the public good.

"He has forbidden his Governors to pass laws of immediate and pressing importance . . .

"He has refused to pass other laws for the accommodation of large districts of people, unless those people would relinquish the right of representation in the Legislature . . ."

26. How would the list of the king's actions in the Declaration of Independence help persuade individuals and other nations that the American colonies' separation from Great Britain was justified?

   (1) by providing overwhelming proof of the British king's misrule
   (2) by proposing a solution to the colonies' problem with Great Britain
   (3) by evaluating the colonies' chances of success at self-government
   (4) by providing the British king with a list of demands
   (5) by demonstrating the ability of the colonists to rule themselves

27. Based on the three actions quoted above, which of the following did the men who wrote the Declaration assume to be true?

   (1) Government is a necessary evil.
   (2) The less government, the better.
   (3) Proper laws are necessary for a just society.
   (4) A king should have the sole power to make laws.
   (5) Representative democracy cannot exist in a monarchy.

Questions 28 and 29 refer to the information and map below.

In the 2002 elections, Republicans and Democrats won state governors' offices as shown in the map below.

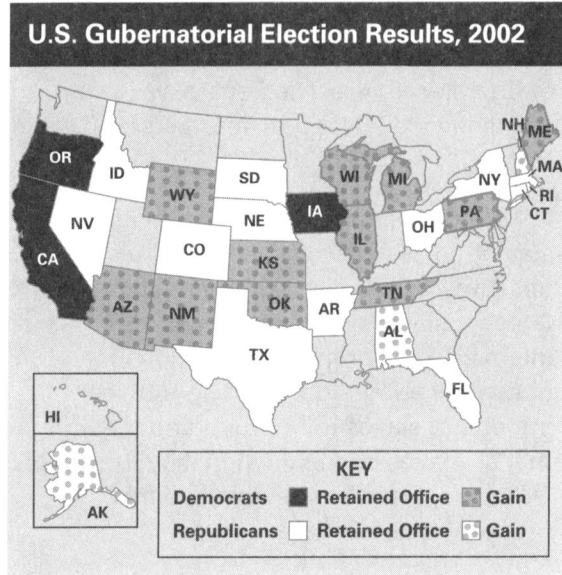

28. In which of the following states did a Democrat gain the governor's office?

   (1) Alabama
   (2) Florida
   (3) Texas
   (4) Arizona
   (5) California

29. Which conclusion is supported by the information from the map?

   (1) Nationwide, there are more Democratic than Republican governors.
   (2) Nationwide, there are more Republican than Democratic governors.
   (3) The governor's office and state legislature are usually controlled by the same party.
   (4) In 2002, there were elections for governor in all 50 states.
   (5) In 2002, the Democrats gained more governorships than the Republicans.

30. During the Great Depression, President Franklin Roosevelt thought that the government needed to use tremendous power to solve the nation's economic problems. He proposed and Congress passed "New Deal" legislation. These laws provided jobs, loans, and subsidies and regulated some industries. They greatly extended the power of the national government. In fact, the Supreme Court ruled that many New Deal laws went beyond the power of the government to regulate commerce. The Court's "hands-off" attitude toward the economy was reflected in its ruling many New Deal laws as unconstitutional.

    Why did the Supreme Court's attitude toward the economy differ from that of President Roosevelt and Congress?

    (1) The Court's main concern was to ensure the Constitution was followed.
    (2) The Court wanted the economy to be regulated at the international level.
    (3) The Court thought the nation's economic problems were not serious.
    (4) The Court's attitude was anti-executive and anti-legislative.
    (5) The bad economy did not personally affect the Supreme Court justices.

31. Although globalization of trade has been the trend in recent years, many nations still resort to protectionism. Protectionist measures limit or exclude imported goods or give advantages to home industries in order to protect employment at home.

    Which is an example of protectionism?

    (1) negotiating a free trade agreement
    (2) giving tax breaks to a domestic industry
    (3) regulating international air flights
    (4) standardizing cargo containers at ports
    (5) importing more goods than are exported

Questions 32 and 33 refer to this chart.

Number of Local Government Units, 1952 and 2002

Type of Government	1952	2002
County	3,052	3,034
Municipal	16,807	19,431
Township and town	17,202	16,506
School district	67,355	13,522
Special district	12,340	35,356
Total Local	116,756	87,849

Source: U.S. Census Bureau

32. What was the primary cause of the decline in the total number of local government units?

    (1) a decrease in the number of county governments
    (2) a decrease in the number of townships and towns
    (3) the consolidation of school districts
    (4) the growth of the urban population
    (5) an increase in the number of special districts

33. What can you conclude about counties from the data in the chart?

    (1) Counties do not lose population as towns and cities do.
    (2) Counties are the most stable units of local government.
    (3) Each county has its own special district.
    (4) Counties have the fewest elected officials of the government units shown.
    (5) Each county has only a single school district.

Questions 34 and 35 refer to this timeline.

U.S. Imperialism, 1893 – 1902	
1893	U.S. overthrows Queen Liliuokalani of Hawaii and sets up new government
1898	Spanish-American War begins; battle for Spanish colonies of Cuba and the Philippines
1899	Philippine revolt against U.S.; U.S. issues Open Door notes to prevent further European partition of China
1900	Boxer Rebellion in China against foreigners
1901	U.S. gains right to two naval stations on Cuba and to send troops if needed
1902	Philippine revolt crushed by U.S.

34. What is wrong with the conclusion that the United States issued the Open Door notes as a result of the Boxer Rebellion?

   (1) The Open Door notes were ineffective.
   (2) The Open Door notes caused the Boxer Rebellion.
   (3) The Open Door notes went to Spain.
   (4) The Open Door notes were aimed at European powers.
   (5) The Open Door notes were issued before the Boxer Rebellion.

35. Which information on the timeline supports the conclusion that the United States won the Spanish-American War?

   (1) The U.S. overthrew the queen of Hawaii in 1893.
   (2) The Spanish-American War began in 1898.
   (3) U.S. Open Door notes of 1899 warned against partitioning China.
   (4) The Philippines started a revolt against the United States in 1899.
   (5) In 1900, the Chinese fought European occupiers during the Boxer Rebellion.

Questions 36 and 37 refer to this paragraph and diagram.

In a market economy, the following economic questions are asked and answered primarily by individuals and companies: What should be produced? How should we produce it? For whom should it be produced?

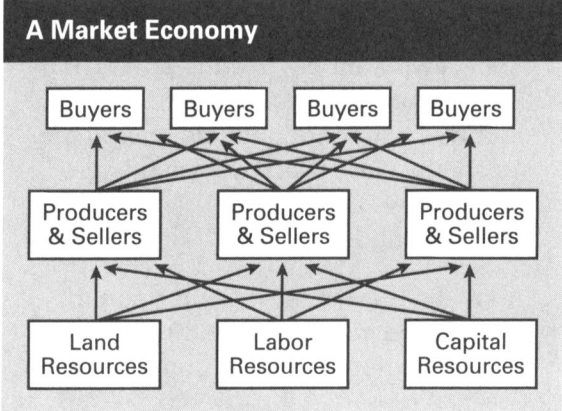

36. What would be a good title for this paragraph and diagram?

   (1) What Buyers Buy
   (2) How Producers and Sellers Affect the Economy
   (3) What Are Economic Resources?
   (4) How Are Resources Allocated?
   (5) How Does a Market Economy Work?

37. Based on the paragraph and diagram, what can you conclude about a market economy?

   (1) The decisions of buyers ultimately influence what is produced.
   (2) Producers make all of the economic decisions.
   (3) Labor is the most important resource.
   (4) The government decides what should be produced.
   (5) All economies are based on the market-economy model.

Questions 38 through 40 refer to this chart.

Population Statistics, by Country, 2001

Country	Birth Rate*	Death Rate*	Life Expectancy at Birth
United States	14.2	8.7	77.3 years
Germany	9.2	10.4	77.6 years
Russia	9.4	13.9	67.3 years
India	24.3	8.7	62.9 years
China	16.0	6.7	71.6 years
Japan	10.0	8.3	80.8 years

* Number of births or deaths during one year for every 1,000 people.
Source: U.S. Census Bureau

38. What was the life expectancy of a baby born in Japan in 2001?

   (1) 10.0 years
   (2) 67.3 years
   (3) 71.6 years
   (4) 77.3 years
   (5) 80.8 years

39. If a nation's death rate exceeds its birth rate, it is losing population. Based on this information and the data in the chart, which nation would you conclude is losing population at the fastest rate?

   (1) United States
   (2) Germany
   (3) Russia
   (4) India
   (5) Japan

40. For which purpose might an international marketing executive use these statistics?

   (1) to identify nations with growing markets
   (2) to identify nations with the largest markets
   (3) to identify nations with culturally diverse markets
   (4) to estimate the overall global market for a product
   (5) to estimate the life expectancy of a product in different markets

Question 41 refers to this cartoon.

Gary Brookins/*Richmond Times-Dispatch* 10/02

41. Which saying BEST restates the main idea of this cartoon about the United Nations?

   (1) Every dog has its day.
   (2) Its bark is worse than its bite.
   (3) Speak softly, but carry a big stick.
   (4) All for one, and one for all.
   (5) The pen is mightier than the sword.

42. In 1823, President Monroe warned that the Americas were no longer open to further colonization by Europe. Any extension of European control in the Americas would be seen as a threat to the United States.

   In which of the following situations did the United States act upon the Monroe Doctrine?

   (1) opening Japan to U.S. trade in 1852
   (2) pressuring the French to end their three-year-old puppet government in Mexico in 1868
   (3) building a transcontinental railroad in 1869
   (4) entering World War I on the side of Great Britain in 1917
   (5) limiting the number of European immigrants entering the United States in 1921

Questions 43 and 44 refer to this map.

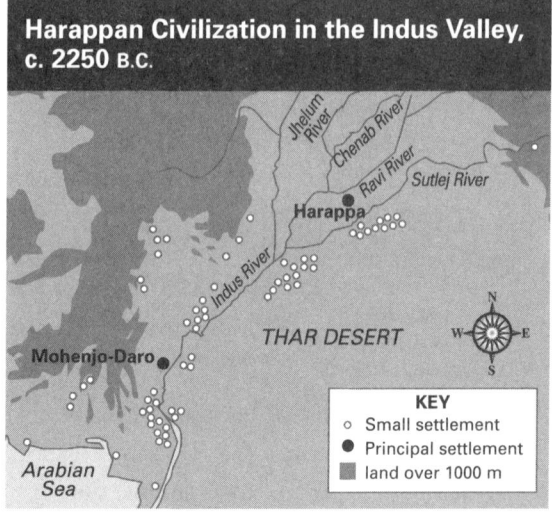

Questions 45 and 46 refer to this paragraph and cartoon.

The government can use fiscal policy to help stimulate or slow the economy. Fiscal policy involves changing the level of taxation or government spending.

HAPPY TRAILS
Ken Davis, Cedartown, Georgia

43. What can you conclude from the information on the map?

(1) People settled near rivers because they provided water for drinking and farming.
(2) The Harappans had a system of flood control.
(3) The two main settlements in the Indus Valley each had more than 30,000 people.
(4) There were many oases in the Thar Desert.
(5) Pieces of inscribed pottery were found at Mohenjo-Daro.

44. To which of the following is the pattern of settlement used by the Harappan civilization MOST similar?

(1) settlement in the cliff dwellings in America's southwestern desert
(2) settlement in the high mountain valleys of ancient Peru
(3) settlement of the Pacific Islands by Polynesians
(4) settlement along the shores of the Mediterranean Sea
(5) settlement along the Nile in ancient Egypt

45. According to the cartoonist, what does President Bush assume will happen as a result of his tax cut?

(1) Government spending will increase.
(2) The economy will slow down.
(3) The economy will be stimulated.
(4) People will have less money to spend.
(5) Voters will be unhappy with his policy.

46. Which image does the cartoonist use to support his conclusion that the tax cut will not work as planned?

(1) President Bush is sitting firmly in the saddle, in control of the economy.
(2) President Bush is looking pleased with his fiscal policy.
(3) The tax cut is represented by a delicious carrot.
(4) The economy is represented by a slow-moving snail.
(5) Fiscal policy is represented by a neat saddle roll.

47. Siberia is a huge region in northeastern Russia. Its climate is cold, even subarctic in places. In 1905, the Trans-Siberian railroad connected the sparsely inhabited, resource-rich Siberia with the more densely populated areas of western Russia.

What was a likely result of the building of the Trans-Siberian railroad?

(1) mining and industrial development in Siberia
(2) establishment of agriculture in Siberia
(3) the relocation of the nation's capital city from western Russia to Siberia
(4) a decrease in Russia's population
(5) Russian emigration to the United States

Question 48 refers to this diagram.

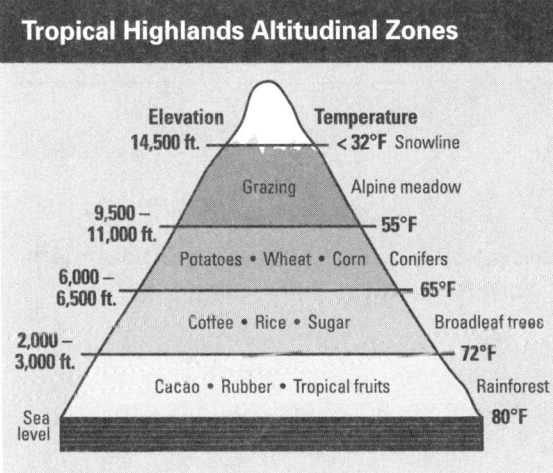

48. Based on the diagram, what is the main cause of changes in vegetation as altitude increases?

(1) lower air pressure
(2) decreased temperature
(3) changes in wildlife
(4) changes in slope
(5) greater distance from the equator

Questions 49 and 50 refer to this excerpt from an Immigration and Naturalization form.

This form is for use to apply to become a naturalized citizen of the United States.

Who May File:

You may apply for naturalization if:
- you have been a lawful permanent resident for five years
- you have been a lawful permanent resident for three years, have been married to a United States citizen for those three years, and continue to be married to that U.S. citizen
- you are the lawful permanent resident child of United States citizen parents
- you have qualifying military service

49. Of the following people who are legally in the United States, who is qualified to apply to become a naturalized citizen?

(1) Lusa, who has been studying in Texas for the past year
(2) Hillaire, who has been working in Maine for the past year
(3) Ali, who has been sightseeing in Colorado for the past three months
(4) Hiroshi, who frequently travels to the United States for business meetings
(5) Carlita, who has been living and working in Ohio for the past six years

50. Which generalization is supported by information from the form?

(1) Marriage to a U.S. citizen shortens the period a person must wait before applying for naturalization.
(2) A person who wants to apply for naturalization should not travel outside the United States.
(3) Noncitizens cannot join the U.S. army.
(4) It takes several years after applying to become a U.S. citizen.
(5) Naturalized citizens have all the rights and privileges of native-born citizens.

Check answers and explanations on page 41.

Step 5: Make Your Plan for Test Success

GED Personal Coach™

You have just finished a full-length Practice GED Social Studies Test. On this page and the next, you will evaluate your results and make a plan to polish up your performance for the actual test.

1. Check your answers starting on page 41. Carefully read the explanation for each correct answer. Use this important feedback to help you understand how to answer GED questions.

2. On the chart below, circle the numbers of the questions that you answered correctly. Add the totals ACROSS for the content areas and DOWN for the thinking skills.

Content Area	Social Studies Thinking Skills				Total Correct
	Comprehension	Application	Analysis	Evaluation	
U.S. History	1, **22**	**23**, 42	2, **9**, **25**, 26, 27, 34	24, 30, **35**	___ out of 13
World History	**41**	8, **44**	18, **43**, 47	11	___ out of 7
Civics & Government	3, **17**, **28**	4, 49	15, 19, **32**, **33**	16, **29**, 50	___ out of 12
Economics	5, **36**	10, 31	**6**, 20, **37**, **45**	21, **46**	___ out of 10
Geography	13, **38**	12, **40**	7, **39**, **48**	14	___ out of 8
TOTALS	___ out of 10	___ out of 10	___ out of 20	___ out of 10	

3. Find two more totals.

    - Count the number of graphic-based questions you got right. Those are the numbers in **bold type** in the chart above. Write that number below.

    Graphic-based questions correct: ___ out of 30

    - Add the Total Correct column to determine how many questions you answered correctly. Write your total below.

    Total Correct: ___ out of 50

4. Use your Total Correct score to determine your readiness to take the actual GED Social Studies Test:

    - If you got **35 or more questions correct,** you should be ready to take the actual Social Studies Test.

    - If you got **30 to 34 questions correct,** you need to brush up on your thinking skills and graphic interpretation skills before you try the test. We recommend the following workbooks available from New Readers Press:

    GED Scoreboost™ Thinking Skills in the Content Areas
    GED Scoreboost™ Graphic Skills in the Content Areas

    - If you got **fewer than 30 questions correct,** you also need to review your social studies materials or ask your teacher for additional social studies materials.

Personal Study Planner

Use your experience with the Practice Test and the evaluation chart on page 38 to answer these questions.

Q: Did you answer all of the questions on the test in 70 minutes?

A: _____

Q: What did you do when you came to a hard question? Did you make your best guess and go on? Or did you spend a lot of time on it before answering it? What do you think you might do differently on the real GED Social Studies Test when you come to a hard question?

A: _____
_____
_____

Q: What was your Total Correct score on the Practice Test? Based on this score, are you ready to take the actual GED Social Studies Test?

A: My score was _____. I am/am not ready to take the GED Social Studies Test. (*Circle one.*)

If you are ready to take the GED Social Studies Test, congratulations! If you are not quite ready yet, continue below.

Q: If you got **fewer than 35 questions correct,** which of the **skills** gave you the most trouble? Look at the chart on page 38 and check off two or three areas below. Ask your teacher to provide you with study materials that will help you strengthen these skills.

	✓	Material Assigned	Pages	Date Finished
Comprehension				
Application				
Analysis				
Evaluation				
Graphics				

Q: If you got **fewer than 30 questions correct,** you also need to develop your **social studies knowledge.** Which of the content areas gave you the most trouble? Check off two or three areas below. Ask your teacher to give you study materials that will help you increase your knowledge.

	✓	Material Assigned	Pages	Date Finished
U.S. History				
World History				
Civics & Government				
Economics				
Geography				

STEP 5

Answers and Bonus Feature

Answers and Explanations

Comprehend What You Read, p. 5

1. **(4) The unemployment rate includes only unemployed people looking for work.** The passage describes which groups of people the Bureau of Labor Statistics counts when tallying the unemployment rate.
2. **(2) The unemployment rate is understated.** Once people give up looking for work, they are no longer counted in the unemployment rate. That means the percentage of unemployed people is actually higher than the unemployment rate indicates.
3. **(2) The Presidential Campaign Organization** The passage describes the makeup of a typical presidential campaign organization, indicating the roles of several of the major types of workers.
4. **(1) To run a presidential campaign, a candidate must have a lot of money.** An organization with several hundred paid workers and thousands of unpaid workers needs a lot of money to function. In addition to paying for labor, the campaign organization pays for traveling, advertising, polling, and so on.

Apply What You Learn, p. 7

1. **(1) refusing to pay taxes** The tactics of civil disobedience are nonviolent, but they are generally against the law. In the United States, refusal to pay taxes is a nonviolent form of protest that is illegal.
2. **(5) the U.S. Civil Rights movement** Martin Luther King, Jr., and his followers were strongly influenced by Gandhi's campaigns of civil disobedience, both in South Africa, as described in the passage, and later in India. They used some similar tactics of civil disobedience, including holding protest marches without permits and taking seats at segregated restaurants where they were not permitted.
3. **(1) a topographic map** A topographic map of the Adirondack Mountains would show land contours and elevations. This information is useful for mountain climbers.
4. **(3) a geologic map** A geologic map shows the composition and distribution of Earth's materials, such as gold and other minerals; it also shows geologic formations in which such deposits are likely to be found. For these reasons, geologic maps are useful for prospectors.

Analyze What You Read, p. 9

1. **(3) to reassure citizens that the state is working to keep them safe** The brochure was sent to all citizens as a way of persuading them that the state government was taking an active role to protect them in case of bioterrorism.
2. **(4) It is possible to contain an attack.** The strategies chosen by the state involve helping victims and stopping the spread of germs in the event of a bioterrorism attack.
3. **(5) Villeneuve should not give his restaurant an English name.** Of all the choices, this is the only opinion, or belief; the other statements are all facts stated in the passage.
4. **(3) He came to appreciate tolerance for the use of different languages.** The controversy over the name of his restaurant led Villeneuve to recall living in Switzerland, where the attitude toward language is less emotional than it is in Quebec. Living in Switzerland allowed Villeneuve to realize that the use of different languages need not be a reason for people to get angry at one another and that tolerance of different languages is an important goal.

Evaluate What You Read, p. 11

1. **(3) The nation needs to move on.** These pardons involved politicians and others caught up in divisive political scandal or crime. When such people are pardoned, the justification is that it is time to heal past wounds and move on.
2. **(1) the Veterans of Foreign Wars** This organization is made up of veterans, including Vietnam War veterans. A large number of members of the VFW were resentful of the leniency granted to people who left the country to avoid being drafted.
3. **(5) Adams had an idealistic view of the Revolution's goals, and Burgoyne had a negative view of its means.** Adams's view of the Revolution was that it was a necessary means to gain freedom and representative government. Since the British general did not have this vision of the future in mind, he tended to focus on the negative aspects of the war that he witnessed, including confiscation of property and persecution of individuals.

Read Timelines, Charts, and Diagrams, p. 13

1. **(3) 43%** (Comprehension) Find "Estuaries" in the first column, then read across the row until you get to the column labeled "Polluted." The figure there is 43%.
2. **(4) the shores of the Great Lakes** (Analysis) Industrial development is one of the major sources of water pollution. Look for the water body with the highest percentage in the "Polluted" column. The Great Lakes shores have the highest percentage of water pollution at 96%.
3. **(3) through selection by the whole Diet** (Comprehension) Follow the arrow pointing to the prime minister to see how the person who fills this office is chosen. The diagram indicates that the prime minister is chosen by the Diet.
4. **(5) Congress** (Application) The Diet is the Japanese legislature, similar to our Congress. Like our Congress, the Diet has two parts, or houses.
5. **(1) The Emperor has little real power.** (Evaluation) The diagram indicates that the Emperor is a figurehead. He has no direct power over the prime minister, the cabinet, or the legislature.

Read Graphs, p. 15
1. **(1) 1992** (Comprehension) The highest point on the trend line, 1992, represents the highest voter turnout, just over 60%.
2. **(2) 1992, 1996, and 2000** (Analysis) These years had the highest voter turnout and were presidential election years. There is a presidential election every four years.
3. **(3) 19.5%** (Comprehension) Look for the portion of the graph that represents annual household income from $50,000 to $74,999. According to the graph, 19.5% of U.S. households had annual income in that range in 1999.
4. **(5) Almost 60% of U.S. households had an income less than $50,000.** (Evaluation) The graph indicates that 28.7% of households had an annual income less than $24,999. Another 29.3% had an annual income between $25,000 and $49,000. Together, they made up almost 60% of U.S. households.

Read Editorial Cartoons and Photos, p. 17
1. **(3) the legislative branch of government** (Comprehension) The cartoon depicts the results of midterm elections (congressional elections that occur halfway through a presidential term) in 2002. Thus, the seesaw represents the legislative branch of government, and the balance of power there has shifted decisively to the Republicans (represented by the elephant in this and many other cartoons).
2. **(1) The Republicans won many of the midterm elections.** (Analysis) The cartoon shows the elephant, representing the Republicans, overpowering the Democrats on the seesaw so much that the Democrats are being shot into the air, representing their ejection from Congress. This indicates that the Republicans won many of the midterm elections and have a majority in both houses of Congress, shifting the balance of power squarely to their party.
3. **(4) In 1911, women in New York still did not have the right to vote.** (Comprehension) States had the power to determine who was eligible to vote unless the Constitution indicated otherwise. Thus, in 1911, women in New York were still fighting for the right to vote, even though women in Wyoming had had that right for over 40 years.
4. **(1) Some state voting laws became unconstitutional.** (Analysis) Once the Constitution granted women the right to vote, the federal law superseded any state law that said they were ineligible to vote.

Read Maps, p. 19
1. **(1) in northern India** (Comprehension) To find the place where Buddhism originated, locate the source of the arrows. It is Thanesar in northern India.
2. **(2) Buddhism spread on Asia's mainland.** (Evaluation) The arrows on the map indicate that Buddhism spread over land, not by sea. It was generally spread by missionaries, travelers, and traders traveling the Silk Roads between China, India, and Central Asia.
3. **(4) Thebes** (Comprehension) According to the map key, cities represented by the smallest dot have a population less than 50,000. Of the cities listed, only Thebes falls in this category.
4. **(3) along the Nile River** (Analysis) If you study the map, you will first see that almost all of Egypt's cities are along the Nile River. In addition, most of the rest of the country is desert with a few oases. There are no cities in the oases. From these facts, you can conclude that most of the population lives along the Nile.

Determine Your Test-Taking Style, pp. 20–21
1. **(5) The Amendment Process** (Comprehension) A good title covers the main idea of the text and diagram. In this case, the main idea is that the Constitution includes a process for its own amendment.
2. **(4) The Constitution should be hard to amend.** (Analysis) The provisions for proposing an amendment show that more than a majority of Congress or a national convention is required. Likewise, in the ratification process, more than a majority is required. These requirements make it difficult to pass an amendment. The framers assumed that this was a good thing; they didn't want the Constitution changed unless the change was so necessary that many people could agree on it.
3. **(4) Haiti** (Comprehension) To find the answer, you need to read the labels on the map until you find the one that indicates U.S. occupation in the years from 1915 to 1934. The place so labeled on the map is Haiti.
4. **(1) U.S. occupation of Afghanistan and Iraq** (Application) The use of force in foreign policy was characteristic of Theodore Roosevelt's administration. It is similar to the policy of intervening in nations thought to harbor terrorists or to be a threat to the U.S.

Practice GED Social Studies Test, pp. 26–37
1. **(4) The transaction was unfair to the island people.** (Comprehension) In the first sentence, Columbus indicates that he had a favorable impression of the generosity of the people of the island of San Salvador. Based on this information, you can infer that Columbus thought exchanging less than a penny for 25 pounds of spun cotton took advantage of that generosity.
2. **(5) He had almost achieved his goal of reaching eastern Asia.** (Analysis) From the last sentence of the quote, you can tell that Columbus assumed that Japan, in eastern Asia, was nearby. He didn't realize that he had landed on islands in the Caribbean Sea, thousands of miles from eastern Asia.
3. **(4) Bill Clinton** (Comprehension) The last column of the chart indicates the age at which each person became president. Find the lowest age. It is 46; then read across the row to the first column to find which person was this age. It was Bill Clinton.

4. **(2) an ambitious, young politician planning his or her political career** (Application) By studying the backgrounds of the recent presidents, a young politician can see possible career paths for reaching high political office. For example, four of the five recent presidents listed in the chart were state governors, suggesting that a governorship might be a more promising career path for presidential hopefuls than a seat in the U.S. Congress.
5. **(4) computer support specialist** (Comprehension) Check the graph's key to see how occupations requiring an associate's degree are marked. Then look for these occupations on the graph; there are two—registered nurses and computer support specialists. *Registered nurses* is not among the choices, but *computer support specialist* is.
6. **(3) Jobs with no educational requirements usually do not pay well or offer good opportunities for advancement.** (Analysis) Although food service jobs will be plentiful during the time period shown on the graph, that alone doesn't make them a good choice for Lester's long-term career. Usually, jobs that require some education provide higher salaries, better benefits, and more chances for advancement.
7. **(2) by showing how happy and healthy a couple with one child is** (Analysis) The billboard shows a happy couple with a happy child who is greeting a kind, authoritative man, presumably a government official. The people are attractive and the message is upbeat. All of this is designed to show the "one couple, one child" policy in a positive light, persuading people to comply.
8. **(5) the Internet stock boom and bust of the 1990s** (Application) The Dutch "tulip mania" of the 1600s is an example of a speculative "bubble" in which the price of a certain type of investment increases rapidly and then falls sharply. In the 1990s, Internet dot.com stocks were very popular and many people bought them, driving prices up sharply. When it became apparent that many of the dot.coms could not make money, people sold their stock, and stock prices plummeted.
9. **(5) Mexicans and Cubans account for about one-third of foreign-born residents.** (Analysis) According to the graph, 27.6% of foreign-born residents in the United States come from Mexico; 3.4% come from Cuba. Together they make up about one-third of all foreign-born residents, at 31% of the foreign-born population.
10. **(1) a printing press** (Application) A printing press is used to manufacture books, magazines, and other publications. Of all the items listed, it is the only one used in the production of another product, which is the defining characteristic of a capital good.
11. **(4) observations of modern Paleolithic groups that survived into modern times** (Evaluation) According to the passage, some Paleolithic cultures persisted into modern times, and their way of life was observed by anthropologists. These observations of people could provide clearer, and thus, better evidence of a division of labor according to gender than the few tools, abstract designs on weapons, and cave paintings of game animals that have survived from prehistoric Paleolithic peoples.
12. **(3) the interstate highway system** (Application) The interstate highway system is part of the U.S. transportation infrastructure, which also includes airports, ports, train systems, and so on.
13. **(3) Asia** (Comprehension) Find 2020 on the horizontal axis. The region with the highest projected energy consumption for 2020 has the highest point on the graph for that year. Find the highest point. The label for the trend line that includes that point is Asia.
14. **(2) declined by about 20 quadrillion BTUs between 1990 and 1999** (Evaluation) This is the only decline shown on the graph. This decline, which, according to the question, coincided with a decline in industrial production, supports the conclusion that industrial production and energy use are linked.
15. **(5) The Constitution should be amended to allow appointments to the House in case of the death of representatives.** (Analysis) Of all the choices, this is the only opinion—a belief that may or may not be true. In the passage, the phrase "some lawmakers think" signals that this idea is an opinion, as does the word *should* in choice (5).
16. **(1) law and order** (Evaluation) People who favor this amendment are concerned that chaos might ensue if many members of Congress died in a short period of time. From their point of view, the proposed amendment would help maintain law and order during a national emergency.
17. **(1) Ensuring a Working House of Representatives** (Comprehension) This is the purpose of the proposed amendment, which is the central topic of the passage. Note that choice (2) is too broad to be a good title.
18. **(2) resentment in Germany over harsh treatment** (Analysis) The clause blaming Germany for all the losses and damages resulting from World War I caused resentment among most Germans. In addition, the reparations, or payments for damages, that the Allies forced Germany to pay were so high that they crippled Germany's postwar economy. This caused even more bitterness and resentment among the Germans.
19. **(4) The school crossing guards are a luxury.** (Analysis) In the passage, the phrase "according to the mayor" signals that the mayor's opinion about the issue is being presented. The mayor calls the crossing guards "a luxury." This is a second signal that the mayor's statement, and choice (4), is an opinion; calling something a luxury is a value judgment, and value judgments are almost always opinions.

20. **(4) During a recession, effective demand for luxury products decreases.** (Analysis) A recession is a period of decreased economic activity often characterized by high unemployment. During such a period, the effective demand for luxury goods drops, since many people can no longer afford them.
21. **(3) Women spend more years in retirement than men.** (Evaluation) The graph shows that, for each country, the bar representing women's years of retirement is longer than the bar representing men's years of retirement. This leads to the conclusion that women spend more years in retirement than men do. Note that you cannot tell why from the graph. It may be that women live longer, that they retire earlier, or some combination of these two factors, but the graph doesn't give enough information to determine the reason.
22. **(1) Maryland** (Comprehension) Check the map key to see how slave states are shown. They are dark green. Of the states listed, only Maryland is dark green, and, therefore, it is the only slave state.
23. **(2) North and South Vietnam in the 1960s, divided by economic and political differences** (Application) The sectional division in the United States was based on differences in the slave states' and free states' economies. The slave states, unlike the free states, were extremely dependent on slave labor in their agricultural economies. Economic differences were also one important cause of the rift between North and South Vietnam. The North had a communist economy, and the South, a capitalist economy.
24. **(5) There were 12 free states and 12 slave states.** (Evaluation) The passage indicates that part of the compromise was admitting Missouri as a slave state and Maine as a free state, effectively canceling out any advantage to either faction. If you count the slave states and free states on the map, you will see that the balance was maintained at 12 each.
25. **(1) It increased regional, not national, loyalty.** (Analysis) As indicated in the passage, the bitter debate over the admission of Missouri lasted for many months. It reinforced feelings of loyalty to one's own region over loyalty to the common good of the nation.
26. **(1) by providing overwhelming proof of the British king's misrule** (Analysis) By listing more than 25 actions that caused harm to the colonies, America's Founders were providing factual evidence that their case against King George was legitimate. This long list of grievances was meant to persuade both fellow American colonists and foreign nations that America was justified in declaring its independence.
27. **(3) Proper laws are necessary for a just society.** (Analysis) The three actions all involve King George's interference in the colonies' lawmaking processes. In addition, the first of the actions describes laws as being "wholesome and necessary for the public good." From this, you can conclude that the Founders assumed that laws were a good and necessary thing when properly administered.
28. **(4) Arizona** (Comprehension) First check the map key to see how states that gained a Democratic governor are shown. They are green with dark green spots. Then look at the map to identify which of the five choices listed is green with dark green spots. Of the five, only Arizona was a gain for the Democrats.
29. **(5) In 2002, the Democrats gained more governorships than the Republicans.** (Evaluation) The map shows that the Democrats gained the governor's office in 11 states and the Republicans gained the governor's office in only 3 states. Note that you cannot draw any conclusions about the nation as a whole because the map has information about only the governors' races held in 2002.
30. **(1) The Court's main concern was to ensure the Constitution was followed.** (Evaluation) According to the passage, both President Roosevelt and Congress were anxious to do something to improve the economy. Both branches of government took forceful action because the nation's situation was so serious. In contrast, the main role of the Supreme Court is to make sure that the Constitution is upheld.
31. **(2) giving tax breaks to a domestic industry** (Application) When an industry gets tax breaks, its cost of doing business goes down, enabling it to charge less for its products. This gives the industry an advantage in the global marketplace, because it can undersell its competitors.
32. **(3) the consolidation of school districts** (Analysis) According to the chart, the number of school districts fell from 67,355 in 1952 to 13,522 in 2002. Since you can assume that the nation's population increased during this 50-year period, the only possible reason for the decrease in school districts is that school districts became larger during this period. Larger school districts made up of several smaller districts would decrease the overall number of school districts.
33. **(2) Counties are the most stable units of local government.** (Analysis) According to the chart, the number of counties was about the same in 1952 as in 2002. However, during this period, the numbers of other units of local government increased or decreased more sharply.
34. **(5) The Open Door notes were issued before the Boxer Rebellion.** (Analysis) According to the timeline, the Open Door notes were issued in 1899 and the Boxer Rebellion took place in 1900. Therefore, the Open Door notes could not have been issued as a result of the Boxer Rebellion.
35. **(4) The Philippines started a revolt against the United States in 1899.** (Evaluation) According to the timeline, the Spanish-American War was over the Spanish colonies of Cuba and the Philippines (1898). In 1899, the Philippines revolted against its new occupier, the United States. This is evidence that the United States won the Spanish-American War.

36. **(5) How Does a Market Economy Work?** (Comprehension) The paragraph describes the basic questions answered by individuals and companies in a market economy, and the diagram shows the relationships among buyers, producers and sellers, and resources in a market economy. The title encompasses this topic and is neither too broad nor too narrow.

37. **(1) The decisions of buyers ultimately influence what is produced.** (Analysis) In the diagram, the arrows point from resources directly to producers and sellers, and from producers and sellers directly to buyers. There are no other institutions involved in making the economic decisions of what is produced and for whom. Therefore, you can conclude that buyers ultimately influence what is produced; through their purchasing decisions, buyers favor particular goods and services of certain producers and sellers. This in turn leads producers and sellers to produce more of the goods and services that buyers favor.

38. **(5) 80.8 years** (Comprehension) Locate Japan in the first column. Then read across the row to the "Life Expectancy at Birth" column. The figure there, 80.8 years, is the number of years a Japanese baby born in 2001 would be expected to live.

39. **(3) Russia** (Analysis) According to the information in the question stem, when the death rate is greater than the birth rate, a nation is losing population. The chart shows that Germany and Russia each have higher death rates than birth rates, so both these nations are losing population. Since the gap between birth rate and death rate is larger for Russia (4.5 more deaths than births per 1,000 people) than for Germany (1.2 more deaths than births per thousand), Russia is the nation losing population at the fastest rate.

40. **(1) to identify nations with growing markets** (Application) An international marketing executive is interested in selling more products abroad. Therefore, he or she is interesting in nations with a growing number of potential customers. The statistics in this chart can help the executive identify nations with growing populations. Nations with higher birth rates than death rates have growing populations.

41. **(2) Its bark is worse than its bite.** (Comprehension) In the cartoon, the United Nations (UN) is represented by a small yapping dog that has little power. Instead, the dog relies on signs that exaggerate its powers to keep visitors in line. The saying "Its bark is worse than its bite" sums up this cartoonist's view of the UN.

42. **(2) pressuring the French to end their three-year-old puppet government in Mexico in 1868** (Application) A puppet government is one that is put in place, not by the nation under its jurisdiction, but by another power or nation. The United States interpreted the French rule of Mexico via a puppet government as an attempt to extend French control in the Americas. It therefore took action according to the Monroe Doctrine to prevent this and pressured the French to end their rule in Mexico.

43. **(1) People settled near rivers because they provided water for drinking and farming.** (Analysis) Settlement along a river was a common pattern in the earliest farming civilizations. The fresh water of a river provided both drinking water and water for crops. The map shows that almost all of the Harappan settlements were on or near the Indus River or its tributaries.

44. **(5) settlement along the Nile in ancient Egypt** (Application) The map shows the Harappan settlements clustering along the banks of the Indus River and its tributaries. This is similar to the Egyptian pattern of settlement along the Nile River. Choice (4) is incorrect because, although the Mediterranean Sea, like the Indus River, is a body of water, the Mediterranean has salty water, not fresh water, and the land along its banks, unlike the land along the Indus, is not necessarily arable (fit to grow crops).

45. **(3) The economy will be stimulated.** (Analysis) The cartoonist shows President George W. Bush (identified by the *W* on his saddle) holding out the tax-cut carrot as a lure in front of the economy (the snail is labeled *Economy*) and saying "Giddy up!" In this way, the cartoonist indicates that the president expects that the tax cut will speed up the sluggish economy.

46. **(4) The economy is represented by a slow-moving snail.** (Evaluation) By showing the economy as a snail, the cartoonist indicates that he thinks the tax cuts will not effectively stimulate the economy.

47. **(1) mining and industrial development in Siberia** (Analysis) With a railroad to transport people, raw materials, and goods to and from distant Siberia, it became possible for Russia to develop the region.

48. **(2) decreased temperature** (Analysis) According to the diagram, the temperature decreases with altitude in the tropical highlands. Temperature affects the type of vegetation that grows in each zone.

49. **(5) Carlita, who has been living and working in Ohio for the past six years** (Application) According to the form, people who are permanent residents can apply for naturalized citizenship. Carlita has been living in Ohio for six years—more than the five-year minimum. Therefore, she is qualified to apply for naturalization. None of the other choices describes people who have been in the United States for a long enough period of time, either as residents or not, to qualify for naturalization.

50. **(1) Marriage to a U.S. citizen shortens the period a person must wait before applying for naturalization.** (Evaluation) According to the "Who May File" list, a person married to a U.S. citizen has to have lived in the United States for only three years before applying for naturalization. In contrast, a noncitizen resident who is not married to a citizen must live here for at least five years before applying for naturalization.